# Unveiling the Mysteries of The Blood of Jesus Christ

## There is still Power in the Blood of Jesus

## Rev. Rudolph K. Roberts

PRESS

# DEDICATION

This book is dedicated to the memory of two of the finest men that I have had the privilege to know.

These men are my biological father, Rev. Zephaniah Roberts, and my spiritual father, Rev. Dr. E.L. Terry.

Rev. Zephaniah Roberts was the greatest father any child could have. He was simply committed to His God and his family.

Rev. Dr. E.L. Terry became my spiritual father in June of 1987. He simply loved me as if I were his own son.

Rev. Zephaniah Roberts
February 16, 1935 – December 23, 1996

Rev. Dr. E.L. Terry
April 29, 1932 – April 14, 2007

They were my best friends.
May their souls rest in peace.

# ACKNOWLEDGEMENTS

I want to first and foremost thank God my Heavenly Father, for sending His only Son Jesus Christ to purchase my full redemption.

I thank God for the person of the Holy Spirit, who really is all to me that Jesus said He would be. He is truly my best friend. It is so true that without the Holy Spirit one can not be drawn to God; one will not have the passion for His people. He is the only one who reveals who God is and what God means by the things He says.

I want to acknowledge my wife Lady Enid Roberts and our six children: Rudeco, Zonovia, Rhema, Rumah, Reuel, and Rudiel for continuing to allow me to spend long hours with God in prayer and studying His word.

The inspiration that comes from my mother encouraging me to be faithful to God is beyond description. Mother Laura Roberts, my (Mom) continues to say in all situations, "God will fix it."

A special thank you to my biological father, the late Rev. Zephaniah Roberts, who discovered the many talents that I was blessed with. He initiated my musical career and was such a driving force behind my early spiritual development. He became the first Associate Minister at the Whole Man Christian Center, the church that I pastor. He was my best friend, and we believed in each other. (Thanks Dad.)

I would also like to thank my office staff secretaries, Mrs. Stella Pinder, for the long hours of typing and editing and Minister Dower Bullard for their untiring work on this project.

Acknowledgement also goes to Ms. Debbie Bannister and Dr. Coralee S. Kelly for the long hours of editing and encouragement. To the members of The Whole Man Christian Center for your continued support over the years; I would like to say a heartfelt "Thank you!"

Thank you to my Spiritual Mentor and father, the late Rev. Dr. E. L. Terry for his spiritual guidance, encouragement, care and love for me. I thank Pastor Mickey Tomberlin for his forward and for becoming my covenant brother. I also thank Apostle Herb Strickland for his foreword and continued friendship and support over the years.

# TABLE OF CONTENTS

# PREFACE

The greatest failure in our churches today is the lack of knowledge.

*"My people are destroyed for lack of knowledge: because thou hast rejected knowledge, I will also reject thee, that thou shalt be no priest to me: seeing thou hast forgotten the law of thy God, I will also forget thy children." (Hosea 4:6)*

The word 'knowledge' has many definitions. According to Webster's dictionary, it is defined as direct perception, understanding acquaintance with practical skill information learning, or well informed. I like all of the explanations, but I believe knowledge is never completed until you get the precept of a thing or place, and make it practical accordingly. The prophet Daniel had many visions and was given many interpretations, but at the closing of his book, as he began to see the events that were going to take place at the end, he wanted to know the meaning of all the things that he saw. However, he was asked to close his book and was promised that knowledge was going to increase.

*"But thou, O Daniel, shut up the words, and seal the book, even to the time of the end: many shall run to and fro, and knowledge shall be increased." (Daniel 12:4)*

I believe that we have already seen this, especially over the last one hundred years. We will see a continual growth in knowledge all over the world. As a musician, I have been recording gospel music for over three decades. When I started, we were still producing records on wax form. Eventually, we went from waxed records played on a turn-table to cassettes, then on to compact discs, and now to the digital and computer age.

We have all benefited from this wealth of knowledge that has spread to the world. In the same way, God promised that there will be an increase of the knowledge of who He is.

*"They shall not hurt nor destroy in all my holy mountain: for the earth shall be full of the knowledge of the LORD, as the waters cover the sea." (Isaiah 11:9)*

This prophecy will be in its fullness when we take the gospel of Jesus Christ to the Jewish nation and fulfil what God had declared in His word.

*"Brethren, my heart's desire and prayer to God for Israel is, that they might be saved. For I bear them record that they have a zeal of God, but not according to knowledge. For they being ignorant of God's righteousness, and going about to establish their own righteousness, have not submitted themselves unto the righteousness of God." (Romans 10:1-3)*

Even though this statement and prophecy was about Israel, I believe that they are suitable for the church of today. Knowledge is more than knowing the words of a passage of scripture. It is more than remembering or retaining the same. Full knowledge is to know what it says, understanding its meaning, and making it applicable in order to get the intended results. God again said through His prophet Isaiah,

*"Whom shall he teach knowledge? And whom shall he make to understand doctrine? Them that are weaned from the milk, and drawn from the breasts.*

*For precept must be upon precept, precept upon precept; line upon line, line upon line; here a little, and there a little: for with stammering lips and another tongue will he speak to this people. To whom he said, this is the rest wherewith ye may cause the weary to rest; and this is the refreshing: yet they would not hear. But the word of the LORD was unto them precept upon precept, precept upon precept; line upon line, line upon line; here a little, and there a little; that they might go, and fall backward, and be broken, and snared, and taken." (Isaiah 28:9-13)*

Again, people are destroyed because of the lack of knowledge. There are many interpretations of scriptures by thousands of persons, yet the Bible says that there are no private interpretations.

There are many concepts, but only one original precept. A precept exists before a concept, therefore, we can have a concept about something, but this may or may not be the original idea.

The Body of Christ is on different levels at different segments. You may find one congregation experiencing more from God than the other congregation. Since God is no respecter of person, I believe this happens simply because God cannot change. It is only when we carry out the original plan of God for a thing that He releases the next stage. Remember there is no limit to God.

In this book about the blood of Jesus, I am placing myself as a lawyer presenting a case that would explain why there is still power in the blood of Jesus, and why the church should return to the importance of the application of the blood of Jesus for today's battles. You will find in this book certain areas of the blood of Jesus that may have been previously overlooked.

# FOREWORDS

In 1987, I met a young man whom I saw a fire burning within. Some fires need to be controlled in order to sustain their true calling in the ministry. It was then in Freeport, Bahamas, that I met that young man named Rudy Roberts. An outstanding singer and songwriter, he never needed me to assist in his ministry, but I asked him to join my ministry and travel fulltime with me in my meetings. He traveled with my son and me for three years and assisted in ministering in song and whatever capacity I needed. Rudy burned within wanting to know more about God's plan for his life. I encouraged Rudy to return to his hometown of Freeport and start the vision God gave to him.

On the 25th day of April 1988, The Rev. Rudolph K. Roberts offices were officially opened. On January 28, 1990, the Whole Man Christian Center was started. He has been founder and pastor of Whole Man Christian Center (WMCC) for over nineteen years, continuing the call of God on his life. It has been my privilege to minister in his church on many occasions and to see the fire continue to burn and grow.

Rev. Roberts was at a restoration conference in Ohio when the Lord spoke to him about the subject of The Blood. He has been teaching on this subject for close to 20 years and has been writing this book for more than 10 years. Rudy's ministry is one of great importance to me and my family. My wife, Nolie and I consider him as one of our sons. The fire that is within Rudy has moved all across his nation and abroad. He ministers tirelessly and continues to stoke the fire. The fire that is within Rudy is the Son of God. I ask you to read this book and let the Son light of God shine upon your hearts. My words to Rudy, I ask him never hide this Son light but let it shine to all who will see.

Dr. E. L. Terry
as told to
Miriam J. Terry

From the very first time I met Brother Roberts over nineteen years ago it became evident that he has a passion for the Blood of Christ that flows out of his spirit. The insight that God has given him has now been extended to us.

Brother Roberts is a man of vision, faith, and integrity. The Apostolic anointing that God has placed upon him reaches far beyond the Bahamas. I believe the experiences that God has allowed in Brother Roberts' life have helped equip him to pour into the lives of those serving in Ministry as well as the Body of Christ.

The church has yet to experience the passion that will be imparted into their lives through Brother Roberts. His voice, like his passion, will not be quenched. In a day when much of the church is focused on how to be blessed, how to prosper and what's in it for me, Brother Roberts reminds us, "If it wasn't for the Blood..."

Apostle Herb Strickland
Restoration Ministries
Toledo, Ohio.

The heart of any man is demonstrated by his actions. It is no different for my friend Reverend Rudolph K. Roberts. He is known to many as a man of compassionate action.

He preaches hard – he prays long hours – he is always looking to reach the masses for the Kingdom of God. He truly has a heart for helping people experience a personal relationship with Jesus Christ.

Pastor Rudy Roberts will tell you that meeting people's needs through the power of God is his passion. He knows from experience that anything to be obtained from the Lord must be obtained by faith. Then, "Faith comes by hearing, and hearing by the Word of God." (Romans 10:17)

A person must read, digest, study and obey the words of truth so that he can be complete and perfect, not lacking anything to do the will of God (see 2nd Timothy 3:16, 17).

When Pastor Rudy Roberts preaches, "I want you well", "I want you baptized in the Holy Ghost", or "I want you delivered and financially free", he is really pointing to the Word of God. God is the one who wants you whole in every aspect of your life, and He has provided a beautiful plan systematically throughout the Word of God.

So many people have been praying and waiting for a breakthrough for so long, yet their circumstances remain unchanged. People do not need clichéd answers – they need solid encouragement from the throne room of Heaven.

For as long as I have known Pastor Rudy Roberts, it still amazes me at the revelation that God gives him. I believe when you read this book you will feel the heart from which it was written.

Take your first step toward wholeness through the ministry of this new book.

Foreword from Reverend Mickey W. Tomberlin
House of Worship and Ministries
Jesup, Georgia

# INTRODUCTION

Many people may ask the question, why am I writing about the blood of Jesus, especially since this is my first book. The shortest answer that I can give you is, I am writing *in obedience to the Lord*. God asked me to write about His blood, and release this book as a covering for all the other projects that He will allow me to release.

I remember travelling to Africa in the nineties to preach the gospel. The Spirit of God instructed me to preach my first sermon about the blood of Jesus. He told me that once I did that, I would have the covering needed for the rest of my revival services. To date, these were some of the most powerful services that I have ever experienced in my entire ministry. There were thousands who received salvation, hundreds were healed, numerous demonic manifestations and numerous demons cast out.

In the Bahamas the subject about the blood of Jesus Christ has been given little or no attention. Some years ago, I preached a sermon in the church that I presently pastor called, 'The Blood: Too Old Fashioned for Today.'

The study of the blood of Jesus has always been of interest to me. I discovered that God initially introduced us to the power of the blood from the fall of man, and continued with the blood to our total restoration which was accomplished at the resurrection of Jesus Christ.

A few years ago, I noticed how little the blood of Christ was used by born again Christians, especially young Christians who were not taught the importance of the blood of Jesus. There are people who are born again, but are still not utilizing the fullness of the blood of Jesus Christ.

I hope that the contents of this book will arouse your interest. I have been in the process of writing this book from the early nineties. I revisited the study of the power that is in the blood of Jesus. I found so many truths not yet explained that I have decided to write a book that would open the eyes of believers and unbelievers to the hidden powers in the blood of Jesus Christ.

I believe it was the Holy Spirit who directed me to write this book. Since the inspiration came to write this book, I have written and recorded many songs. The more I researched the blood of Jesus, the clearer it becomes why the Holy Spirit inspired me to write this book. This book will unveil the mysteries of the blood of Jesus that have been hidden for ages, and you will see why Jesus Christ is the volume of the entire book.

When the Israelites went into battle and conducted their battle plans according to the way God instructed them, they won. There has never been a time that they won a battle without applying the blood of Jesus Christ. This clearly shows that there is no victory without the blood of Jesus Christ.

The Bible states that there were times when Israel went into battle and did not follow the instructions of God. During these times, they were defeated. An example of this is in the twentieth chapter of the book of Judges.

The Israelites had to face their own brethren the Benjamites for the sin of sodomy. They lost over forty thousand men because of disobedience to God's instructions to apply the blood first. This has been the pattern from Abel in Genesis to Mary and Joseph in Matthew. God has not changed. As in the case of Job, God required Old Testament saints to apply the blood first in every battle, as well as, for the covering of every family member.

The prophets of old have all done this in faith, but did not receive the promise. According to Hebrews 11, they had faith, but they could not get to the Father without the substitute. They had to wait for the fulfilling of every shadow in the Old Testament, which took place when Jesus Christ was crucified, died, buried, and was resurrected on the third day.

In the book of Revelation when John was on the Isle of Patmos, he was given a revelation from Jesus Christ. This book gives us the condition of the churches in the last days, and the things that would take place on the earth in the last days, and into eternity. John described his setting and the reason why he was there. He also explained who was giving him the revelation. The first statement that was made by Jesus was:-

*"I am Alpha and Omega, the beginning and the ending, saith the Lord, which is, and which was, and which is to come, the Almighty." (Revelation 1:8)*

At the beginning, it was the blood of Jesus that covered man's nakedness. At the conclusion of man's rule, it will be the blood of Jesus that will win man's final battle, the battle of Armageddon.

You will want to read this book, apply its contents to your life and the lives of your family, and I guarantee you will win. Because you are a child of God, when you win you will want others to do likewise.

Read, be blessed, and changed!

# CHAPTER ONE

# UNVEILING THE MYSTERIES OF THE BLOOD OF JESUS

## There Is Still Power In The Blood

In Genesis 3:21, God made coats of animal skin to cover man's nakedness. This is the first record of the shedding of innocent blood in the Bible. God promised there would be a battle between the seed of the woman and the devil. This predicts the defeat of the devil by Jesus Christ. Throughout the Scriptures, God showed us that He does not change. Mysteries are not hidden from us; instead, they are hidden for us.

> *"But we speak the wisdom of God in a mystery, even the hidden wisdom, which God ordained before the world unto our glory: Which none of the princes of this world knew: for had they known it, they would not have crucified the Lord of glory." (1 Corinthians 2:7-8)*

In this passage of Scripture, we are told that the mystery of the cross was hidden from principalities and satan himself. I like to put it this way: the house of Heaven met and God took counsel from Himself.

Only three persons were invited to the meeting — Father, Son, and Holy Spirit. I was invited to the meeting. God did not invite

Gabriel, Michael or lucifer, the three archangels who were next to the Godhead; but He invited me. I accepted the invitation —even though I did not know me— I had a power of attorney in the person of Jesus Christ. He represented me. This is where the mystery of the cross was discussed.

My parents names were selected; and my place, date and time of birth were also decided. If God had told Gabriel, His messenger, He also had to tell Michael, His warrior, and lucifer, His Worship Leader. They were next in line of command in Heaven. If God had told one of the archangels, then He had to tell all three.

According to the word of God spoken through Peter at Cornelius' house, **Acts 10:34**, we are told that God is no respecter of person. Cornelius and his entire household who were Gentiles heard the gospel, received salvation, and the baptism of the Holy Ghost.

> *"But as it is written, eye hath not seen, nor ear heard, neither have it enter into the heart of man, the things which God hath prepared for them that love Him.*
> *But God hath revealed them unto us by His Spirit: for the Spirit searcheth all things, yea the deep things of God. For what man knoweth the things of man save the spirit of man which is in him? Even so the things of God knoweth no man but the Spirit of God." (1Corinthians 2:9-11)*

I believe in order for us to understand the hidden mysteries of the cross, and the power that is in the blood of Jesus, we need a new approach to the study of God's word. There are many traditional views and methods suggested to study God's word. However, I found that the most effective way, and I believe the only accurate way, is to look for Jesus in the whole Bible from Genesis to Revelation.

Throughout the Psalms, King David gave prophecies concerning Jesus Christ, but when he quoted *Psalms 40:7 "Then said I, Lo, I come: in the volume of the book it is written of me"*, he gave the overall picture of who Jesus really is in reference to the Bible. The apostle Paul also got a revelation of who Jesus is.

*"Then said I, Lo, I come in the volume of the book it is written of me, to do thy will, O God." (Hebrews 10:7)*

We need to know that the Old Testament is the New Testament concealed, and the New Testament is the Old Testament revealed. Even the Angels, who are Spirit beings, needed the blood of Jesus Christ to win battles. This is one of the reasons when there was a contention over the body of Moses, Michael told the devil in **Jude verse 9, "The Lord rebuke thee."** When he said this, he incorporated the blood of Jesus in this statement.

*"And all that dwell upon the earth shall worship him, whose names are not written in the book of life of the Lamb slain from the foundation of the world." (Revelation 13:8*

This verse of Scripture tells us that before Christ died, four thousand years after the restoration of the earth, God saw Him slain. This shows the completed work of redemption in the mind of God. It is believed that the prophet Isaiah wrote his book in Palestine about 792-722 B.C. He also had this revelation of the lamb slain from the foundation of the world.

*"Who hath believed our report? And to whom is the arm of the LORD is revealed? For he shall grow up before him as a tender plant, and as a root out of a dry ground; he had no form nor comeliness; and when we shall see him, there is no beauty that we should desire him. He is despised and rejected of men; a man of sorrows, and acquainted with grief: and we hid as if it was our faces from him; he was despised, and we esteemed him not. Surely he hath borne our grief, and carried our sorrows: yet we esteem him stricken, smitten of God and afflicted. But he was wounded for our transgressions; he was bruised for our iniquities: the chastisement of our peace was upon him; and with his stripes we are healed." (Isaiah 53:1-5)*

# FIRST FRUIT OFFERING

Isaiah included himself in the death, burial and resurrection of Jesus Christ. I believe that he was in the firstfruit offering that Christ took to the Father.

*"But now is Christ risen from the dead, and become the firstfruits of them that slept. For since by man came death, by man came also the resurrection of the dead. For as in Adam all die, even so in Christ shall all be made alive." (1 Corinthians 15:20-22)*

Why would the apostle Paul call Jesus the firstfruit of them that sleep? I believe that he through the Holy Spirit was drawing reference to one of the eight feasts of Israel, which were all a shadow of things to come and would all be fulfilled in Jesus. Remember, the whole Bible is about Jesus.

In **Leviticus 23**, there is a listing and explanation of the eight feasts of Israel. I will talk about the feast of Firstfruits. However, in case you are interested in the feasts of Israel or the feasts of Jehovah, they are:-

1) *Weekly Sabbath (Leviticus 23:3; Exodus 20:8-11)*
2) *Feast of Passover (Leviticus 23:4-5; Exodus 12:1-11; Numbers 9:9; 28:16; Deuteronomy 16:1)*
3) *Feast of Unleavened Bread (Leviticus 23:6-8; Exodus 2:15; Numbers28:17; Deuteronomy 16:6)*
4) *Feast of the Firstfruits (Leviticus 23:9-14; Exodus 23:16; Numbers 28:26; Deuteronomy 16:9),*
5) *Feast of Pentecost (Leviticus 23:15-21; Deuteronomy 16:9-12; Acts 2)*
6) *Feast of Trumpets (Leviticus 23-23-25; Numbers 10:1-10; Numbers 29-1-6)*
7) *Feast of the Great Day of Atonement. (Leviticus 16; Leviticus 23:26-32; Numbers 29:7)*
8) *Feast of Tabernacles (Leviticus 23:33-44; Numbers 29:2-40; Deuteronomy 16:13; Zechariah 14:16)*

These Scripture references are not placed here to bore you, but to further reinforce the case that I am making concerning the blood of Jesus Christ. In these feasts, every animal sacrifice that was made represented the death, burial and resurrection of Jesus Christ. Now let us return to the firstfruits and see how Isaiah and the prophets were a part of this. In Hebrews 11, the book that I call *"The Hall of Fame of Faith Walkers"*, we see a listing of many of the Faith giants beginning with Abel.

In this Chapter, we do not see Isaiah the prophet's name, but we believe that he was one of them. It is believed that Isaiah died by being placed in a log of wood and sawn asunder.

I also believe the apostle Paul alluded to this in the book of **Hebrews** which states,

*"They were stoned, they were sawn asunder, were tempted, were slain with the sword: they wandered about in sheep-skins and goatskins; being destitute, afflicted, tormented. Of whom the world was not worthy: they wandered in deserts, and in mountains, and in dens and caves of the earth. And these all having obtained a good report through faith, received not the promise: God having provided some better thing for us, that they without us should not be made perfect." (Hebrews 11:37-40)*

Isaiah, like most of the prophets of the Old Testament, saw the birth, ministry, death, burial, resurrection, and second coming of Jesus Christ.

*"For unto us a child is born, unto us a son is given; and the government shall be upon his shoulder; and his name shall be called Wonderful, Counselor, The Mighty God, The Everlasting Father, The Prince of Peace. Of the increase of his government and peace there shall be no end, upon the throne of David, and upon his kingdom, to order it, and to establish it with judgment and with justice from hence-forth even for ever. The Zeal of the LORD of hosts will perform this." (Isaiah 9:6-7)*

Isaiah, in the preceding passage gave us a prophecy that covers the birth of Jesus unto eternity. Isaiah foretold the Virgin's birth of Christ.

*"Therefore the Lord himself shall give you a sign; Behold, a virgin shall conceive, and bear a son, and shall call his name Immanuel." (Isaiah 7:14)*

This prophecy was fulfilled in *Luke 1:26-31*

*"And in the sixth month the angel Gabriel was sent from God unto a city Galilee, named Nazareth. To a virgin espoused to a man whose name was Joseph, of the house of David; and the virgin's name was Mary. And the angel came in unto her, and said, Hail thou that art highly favoured, the Lord is with thee: blessed art thou among women. And when she saw him, she was troubled at his saying, and cast in her mind what manner of salutation this should be. And the angel said unto her, Fear not, Mary: for thou hast found favour with God. And, behold, thou shalt conceive in thy womb, and bring forth a son, and shalt call his name JESUS."*

In Luke 2:7, we read, *"And she brought forth her firstborn son, and wrapped him in swaddling clothes, and laid him in a manger; because there was no room for them in the inn."*

There are many other prophecies in the book of Isaiah and the prophets that deal specifically with the coming of Jesus Christ, his ministry, death, burial, resurrection and ascension. We will refer to a lot of their writings in later chapters. However, I will take a look at **Psalms 22**. King David starts this chapter by quoting a statement that Jesus would make while He was on the cross.

*"My God, My God, why hast thou forsaken Me? why art thou so far from helping Me, and from the words of My roaring?" (Psalms 22:1)*

This prophecy was fulfilled in **Matthew 27:46** and **Mark 15:34.**

*"And about the ninth hour Jesus cried with a loud voice, saying, Eli, Eli, lama sabachthani? That is to say, My God, My God why hast thou forsaken Me?" (Matthew 27:46)*

Even though Jesus did not speak everything that King David said, we are sure that when He was on the cross and said *"My God, My God why has thou forsaken Me,"* it was a fulfillment to this prophecy. It is important to note that the entire chapter of **Psalms 22** gave approximately thirty facts about the sufferings of the Messiah. Let us examine verse 16 of the same chapter.

*"For dogs have compassed Me: the assembly of the wicked have enclosed Me: they pierced My hands and My feet." (Psalms 22:16)*

This is referring to the Gentiles who were called dogs and who compassed Jesus Christ to crucify Him. This is fulfilled in **Matthew 27:20, "But the chief priests and elders persuaded the multitude that they should ask for Barabbas, and destroy Jesus."**

The apostle Peter also referred to this when he was preaching on the day of Pentecost recorded in **Acts 2:36.**

*"Therefore let all the house of Israel know assuredly, that God hath made that same Jesus, whom ye have crucified, both Lord and Christ."*

After the healing of the lame man at the gate of the temple and Peter had preached his second sermon, five thousand souls were added to the church. This upset the rulers, elders, scribes and the high priests so much that they had Peter and John arrested until the next day. They set them in the midst of the religious leaders and asked them by what power or by what name have they done this? Peter being filled with the Holy Ghost started preaching again. They further threatened them and asked them not to speak or teach in the name of Jesus. They could not find any reason to condemn them because the man who was healed was about forty years of age. They let them go, and they went to their own company and reported all that the chief priests and elders said unto them. When they heard this they all with one accord began to pray.

> *"The kings of the earth stood up, and the rulers were gathered together against the Lord, and against Christ. For of a truth against Thy Holy child Jesus, whom thou hast anointed, both Herod and Pontius Pilate, with the Gentiles, and the people of Israel, were gathered together. For to do whatsoever thy hand and thy counsel determined before to be done.*
>
> *And now, Lord, behold their threatenings: and grant unto thy servants, that with boldness they may speak thy word. By stretching forth thine hand to heal; and that signs and wonders may be done by the name of Thy Holy Child Jesus." (Acts 4:26-30)*

When they got through praying, the place was shaken where they were assembled together, and they were all filled with the Holy Ghost and spoke with boldness.

The blood of Jesus Christ might be old fashioned for today's modern day church, but I am totally convinced that the same way it disturbed the religious folks and the powers of evil during the days of the apostles, if we would believe and go back to the blood of Jesus Christ and apply it to our everyday situations, we will receive the same results.

Going back to Isaiah and the clouds of witnesses, let us revisit **1 Corinthians 15:20.**

> *"But now is Christ risen from the dead, and become the first-fruits of them that slept."*

The term **'*them that slept'*** refers to the great clouds of witnesses that the apostle Paul wrote about.

*"Wherefore seeing we also are compassed about with so great a cloud of witnesses, let us lay aside every weight and the sin which doth so easily beset us, and let us run with patience the race that is set before us. Looking unto Jesus, the author and finisher of our faith; who for the joy that was set before him endured the cross, despising the shame, and is set down at the right hand of the throne of God."* *(Hebrew 12:1-2)*

This Scripture plainly stated that these witnesses faith began and ended in Christ, and so will everyone that will ever get to Heaven.

King David said that Jesus was going into Hell when He died, but God was not going to allow Him to stay or let His body see corruption. **In Psalms 16:10** he wrote,

*"For thou wilt not leave my soul in Hell; neither wilt thou suffer thine Holy One to see corruption."*

He further prophesied in Psalms 68:18.

*"Thou hast ascended on high, thou hast led captivity captive: thou hast received gifts for men; yea, for the rebellious also, that the Lord God might dwell among them."* *(Psalms 68:18)*

King David prophesied this, and the apostle Paul confirmed it in Ephesians 4:7-11.

*"But unto every one of us is given grace according to the measure of the gift of Christ. Wherefore He* **saith, when** *He ascended on high, He led captivity captive, and gave gifts unto men. Now that He ascended, what is it but that He also descended first into the lower parts of the earth? He that descended is the same also that ascended up far above all Heavens, that He might fill all things. And He gave some, apostles; and some, prophets; and some evangelists; and some, pastors and teachers."*

From what we just read, I believe that Jesus went into Hell and defeated the devil and all of his demons. When Jesus was resurrected, He brought with Him those that were in Abraham's Bosom. These were the people who died in faith in the blood of Jesus from Genesis in the Old Testament to the four Gospels (Matthew, Mark, Luke, and John), in the New Testament. These people became the firstfruit offering unto God.

In Colossians, the apostle Paul continues to strengthen his case concerning the victory of Jesus Christ over satan and his demons when He wrote,

> *"Blotting out the handwriting of ordinances that was against us, which was contrary to us, and took it out of the way, nailing it to His cross; And having spoiled principalities and powers, He made a shew of them openly, triumphing over them in it." (Colossians 2:14-15)*

We have to take a look at what Matthew said to further confirm this truth about the resurrection of the firstfruit.

> *"Jesus, when He had cried again with a loud voice, yielded up the ghost. And, behold, the veil of the temple was rent; in twain from the top to the bottom; and the earth did quake, and the rocks rent. And the graves were opened; and many bodies of the saints which slept arose. And came out of the graves after His resurrection, and went into the holy city, and appeared unto many." (Matthew 27:50-53)*

Abraham and the resurrected saints could not meet with the Father until Christ had completed the plan of redemption.

> *"And almost all things are by law purged with blood; and without the shedding of blood there is no remission." (Hebrews 9:22)*

When troubles, disappointments, and sickness come our way and we are faced with battles, satan sends strongmen (principalities) in our lives to make us believe we are not delivered and that we are never going to be set free.

The Lord said to me, "the people in the Body of Christ need to be reminded that there is still power in the blood of Jesus."

A police officer in Freeport asked me, "Do you still believe there is power in the blood of Jesus Christ? How long are you still going to believe this"? I said to him, "Until it has no more power." This will never happen, so I will believe forever.

At times when circumstances, troubles, and frustrations we face in our every day lives surrounds us, we tend to forget that there's still power in the blood of Jesus Christ.

# CHAPTER TWO

# ALL ABOUT JESUS

If we are going to clearly understand the power that is in the blood of Jesus, then we must approach the study of God's word with a new outlook. We must know that the whole Bible is about Jesus Christ. Therefore, since Jesus is the Word then we must recommend that the Old Testament is Jesus Christ concealed, and the New Testament is Jesus Christ revealed.

The first appearance of Jesus Christ in the Bible is at the very beginning of the Scriptures.

*"In the beginning* **God created the Heaven and the Earth."** *(Genesis 1:1)*

The Hebrew word for God is Elohim, which is a singular word with a plural meaning. God the Father, the Commander; God the Son, the Administrator; and God the Holy Spirit, the Manifestor of all that was commanded and administrated.

*God said, "Let us make man in our image, after our likeness: and let them have dominion over the fish of the sea, and over the fowl of the air, and over the cattle, and over all the earth, and over every creeping thing that creepeth upon the earth." (Genesis 1:26)*

The apostle John gives us an even clearer look at who Jesus is when he begins the Gospel of St. John.

> *"In the beginning was the Word, and the Word was with God, and the Word was God. The same was in the beginning with God. All things were made by Him; and without Him was nothing made that was made. In Him was life: and the life was the light of men. And the light shineth in darkness; and the darkness comprehended it not."(John 1:1-5)*

If there is any doubt of who John was talking about, then we need to take a look at the fourteenth verse of St. John. In this verse we will see that the only person who fits this description is Jesus Christ.

> *"And the Word was made flesh, and dwelt among us, (and we beheld His glory, the glory as of the only begotten of the Father,) full of grace and truth."(St. John 1:14)*

The first symbol (Shadow or Type) that represents Jesus is found in Genesis.

> *"And out of the ground made the LORD God to grow every tree that is pleasant to the sight and good for food; The Tree Of Life also in the midst of the garden, and the tree of knowledge of good and* **evil.***" (Genesis 2:9)*

The Tree Of Life is a shadow of the concealed Christ that we mentioned earlier. This Tree Of Life also represents the first mercy seat or the First Ark of the Covenant.

Take note that the Tree Of Life represents Jesus, and the tree of knowledge of good and evil represents choice. Remember lucifer was created to do good but chose to do evil. God drove Adam and Eve out of the garden because after they sinned they could have eaten of the Tree Of Life and live forever.

The first prophecy of the crucifixion of Jesus Christ is also found in **Genesis 3:15.**

*"And I will put enmity between thee and the woman, and between thy seed and her seed; it shall bruise thy head, and thou shalt bruise his heel." (Genesis 3:15)*

This totally confused the devil, because a woman does not have seed. satan did not understand that this seed would have nothing to do with man. When he saw Cain, he thought that he was the promised seed so he caused jealousy to enter into his heart, which drove him to kill his brother Abel.

*"And in the process of time it came to pass, that Cain brought of the fruit of the ground an offering unto the Lord. And Abel, he also brought of the firstlings of his flock and of the fat thereof. And the Lord had respect unto Abel and to his offering: But unto Cain and to his offering He had not respect. And Cain was very wroth, and his countenance fell. And the Lord said Cain, why art thou wroth? And why is thy countenance fallen? If thou doest well, shalt thou not be accepted? And if thou doest not well, sin lieth at the door. And unto thee shall be his desire, and thou shall rule over him. And Cain talked with Abel his brother: and it came to pass, when they were in the field, that Cain rose up against Abel his brother, and slew him. And the Lord said unto Cain, where is Abel thy brother? And he said, I know not: am I my brother's keeper? And He said, what hast thou done? The voice of thy brother's blood crieth unto me from the ground." (Genesis 4:3-10)*

When we look at this story, one may ask what does this have to do with the blood of Jesus.

Let us examine the evidence closely and see what conclusion we can come to. Let us say that the first murder recorded in the Bible was over religion. However, what I am about to say may upset many or many may disagree. Then again, it may help thousands.

I really do not believe in religion. I believe that religion is merely man's search for God; this is the reason why there are so many. Well, one may ask what about Christianity? Even though Christianity is categorized as another religion by the world, to me it is not a religion. It is man's relationship with God through Jesus. I believe that the Bible is the infallible Word of God and Jesus Christ is the only begotten Son of God.

*"For God so loved the world, that He gave His only begotten Son, that whosoever believeth in Him should not perish, but have everlasting life." (St. John 3:16)*

*Jesus saith unto him "I am the Way, the Truth, and the Life; no man cometh unto he Father but by me."(St. John 14:6).*

Jesus answered this question in response to Thomas' question in **St. John 14:5**, *"Thomas saith unto Him, Lord, we know not whither thou goest; and how can we know the way?"*

For us to really get the clear understanding of the fullness of what Jesus was saying, we must take some time to study the Tabernacle that Moses built in the wilderness.

## JESUS THE TABERNACLE IN THE WILDERNESS

This Tabernacle was given to Moses while he was up on Mount Sinai. In **Exodus 24:1-2,** Moses was concluding his fourth ascent in the mountain having made three previous ascents and descents in Chapter Nineteenth. His fourth ascent was in **Exodus 20:21,** and his descent in **Exodus 24:3.**

God instructed Moses to come up unto Him along with Aaron, Nadab, Abihu, and seventy of the elders of Israel, and worship afar off. Moses came down from the mountain and met with the congregation. He wrote all the words of the Lord and built an altar, and made sacrifices unto the Lord.

*"And Moses came and told the people all the words of the Lord, and all the judgments: and all the people answered with one voice, and said, all the words which the Lord hath said will we do. And Moses wrote all the words of the Lord, and rose up early in the morning, and builded an altar under the hill, and the twelve pillars, according to the twelve tribes of Israel. And he sent young men of the children of Israel, which offered burnt offerings, and sacrificed peace offerings of oxen unto the Lord. And Moses took half of the blood, and put it in basons; and half of the blood he sprinkled on the altar. And he took the book of the covenant, and read in the audience of the people: and they said, all that the Lord had said will we do, and be obedient. And Moses took the blood, and sprinkled it on the people, and said, Behold the blood of the covenant, which the Lord hath made with you concerning all these words. Then went up Moses, and Aaron, Nadad, and Abihu, and seventy of the elders of Israel: and they saw the God of Israel: and there was under his feet as it were a paved work of a sapphire stone, and as it were the body of Heaven in His clearness. And upon the nobles of the children of Israel He laid not His hand: also they saw God, and did eat and drink." (Exodus 24:3-11)*

Before Moses and those with him could see or meet with God, they had to offer blood sacrifice. This clearly showed us that there is and never will be any revelation or access to God without the blood of Jesus.

Here Moses saw the pattern of the Tabernacle and the body of Heaven through the bottom of God's feet. The Tabernacle is the Grandfather clause of the entire Bible. It is the pattern by which the whole Bible follows. It is also the shadow of the cross of Jesus Christ who was crucified on the fourth day of man's week of seven days.

If we examine the *'like as principle'* in the Bible, we would find several occurrences.

*"But, beloved, be not ignorant in this one thing, that one day is with the Lord as a thousand years, and a thousand years as one day." (2Peter 3:8)*

*"For a thousand years in thy sight are but as yesterday when it is past, and as a watch in the night." (Psalms 90:4)*

God questioned me on this subject of shadow, and asked me to show Him a shadow from something that is not there. My answer was this was not possible, because to get a shadow you must have an object, and for an object to cast a shadow there must be light. I know I have your attention. Many of you are saying, how he arrived at this conclusion. You may be wondering what does this have to do with the blood of Jesus Christ.

Let us not forget that the Tabernacle and all of its materials were shadows or types that represent Jesus Christ. We also need to bear in mind that everything that we are experiencing today had been finished in God before the foundation of the world.

While in the mountain the materials, pattern and specification, and their consecration were outlined to Moses. These can be seen in **Exodus, Chapter 25 through Chapter 31.**

All seven of these chapters would take a lot of time and space to print. I ask that you take some time to read and study these passages, so that you can get a better understanding of why I am presenting my case concerning the blood of Jesus Christ. If I can get the readers to see Jesus and the power of His blood, then my purpose for writing this book would be accomplished.

The Old Testament materials were shadows of things to come. The New Testament is the substance of the shadows in the Old Testament. Israel is the shadow, and the Church is the substance.

*"Who serve unto the example and shadow of Heavenly things, as Moses was admonished of God when he was about to make the tabernacle: for, see, saith He, that thou make all things according to the pattern shewed to thee in the mount." (Hebrews 8:5)*

I want to remind you that it was said earlier that the whole Bible is about Jesus. Now we must also accept the fact that the types and shadows of the Old Testament are all representing Jesus Christ. With this in mind, let us revisit the Tabernacle that God told Moses to build and the materials he was to use.

My goal here is to show you that every piece of material and furniture portrayed the ministry, the characteristics or the death, burial, and resurrection of Jesus Christ. All the materials were symbols of Heavenly things.

*"And the Lord spoke unto Moses, saying, speak unto the children of Israel, that they bring Me an offering: of every man that giveth it willingly with his heart ye shall take my offering. And this is the offering which ye shall take of them; gold, and silver, and brass, and blue, and purple, and scarlet, and fine linen, and goat's hair, and ram's skins dyed red, and badgers skins, and shittim wood. Oil for the light, spices for anointing oil, and for sweet incense, Onyx stones, and stones to be set in the ephod, and in the breast-plate. And let them make Me a sanctuary; that I may dwell among them. According to all that I shew thee, after the pattern of the tabernacle, and the pattern of all the instruments thereof, even so shall ye make it." (Exodus 25:1-9)*

Let us look at the materials used here and see how they are types or shadows of Jesus Christ.

Gold, speaks of divinity or Jesus Christ the Divine One. There are many Bible facts that we can use to prove that Jesus is the only Divine One. We will refer to one: that He was and still is the only virgin birth recorded in the Bible or any other book. This was prophesied by the prophet Isaiah in **Isaiah 7:14,** and fulfilled in the four gospels: Matthew, Mark, Luke and John.

Silver, this speaks of redemption or Jesus Christ our Redeemer. As was said about the Divine One, there are numerous Scripture references we can use to substantiate His claim as our Redeemer. I would like to draw your attention to a story in **Luke, Chapter Sixteenth.**

This is a beautiful story of a rich man and a beggar named Lazarus. This story shows a contrast between two beggars: one begging on the Earth, and the other begging in Hell. Most people who read their Bibles would know this story, but I want to draw your attention to the place that these two people found themselves after their deaths.

*"And it came to pass, that the beggar died, and was carried by the angels into Abraham's Bosom: the rich man also died, and was buried."* **(Luke 16:22)**

Abraham's Bosom was the name for Paradise or the underworld where all the saints of the Old Testament, who died in faith in the blood of Jesus, were kept.

Every animal sacrifice that these saints made, pointed to the death of Jesus Christ on the cross. These folks needed a Redeemer, which could only take place by the blood of Christ.

*"Christ hath redeemed us from the curse of the law, being made a curse for us: for it is written, curse is every one that hangeth on a tree. That the blessing of Abraham might come to the Gentiles through Jesus Christ: that we might receive the promise of the Spirit through faith." (Galatians 3:13-14)*

Now we see that not even the people who gave us all of the stories in the Old Testament, no matter how faithful they were to God, could be redeemed without the blood of Jesus Christ.

The next material that was used in the tabernacle was brass. Brass is symbolic of the suffering Saviour.

When Jesus was having a discourse with Nicodemus, in **St. John 3:14** he stated, **"And as Moses lifted up the serpent in the wilderness, even so must the Son of man be lifted up."**

For us to get a clear look at why brass represents the suffering Saviour, then we must revisit the travel of the Children of Israel in the wilderness and see what happened to those who were bitten by the fiery serpents.

God was not pleased with His people not showing faith in Him or the leader that He had chosen for them, so He sent fiery serpents among the people. The serpents bit them, and much people of Israel died.

After this was done, the people came to Moses and told him that they sinned and had spoken against God and against him. They asked Moses to pray to God for them and ask Him to take away the serpents. When Moses prayed, God instructed him to make a fiery serpent out of brass and set it upon a pole. Every one that was bitten by a fiery serpent was to look upon this brazen serpent and be healed.

Moses did as God told him and had the people do likewise. All who were bitten by the fiery serpent, when they looked upon the serpent that Moses made, were healed.

*"And the Lord said unto Moses, Make thee a fiery serpent and set it upon a pole: and it shall come to pass, that every one that is bitten, when he looketh upon it, shall live. And Moses made a serpent of brass, and put it upon a pole, and it came to pass, that if a serpent had bitten any man, when he beheld the serpent of brass, he lived." (Numbers 21:8-9)*

Throughout the Bible the serpent is symbolic of sin. Doesn't this make you wonder why God used the symbol of sin to represent Jesus; and when people looked upon it were healed?

*"For even hereunto were ye called: because Christ also suffered for us, leaving us an example, that ye should follow His steps: who did no sin, neither was guile found in His mouth: Who, when He was reviled, reviled not again; when He suffered, He threatened not; but committed Himself to Him that judgeth righteously: Who His own self bare our sins in His own body on the tree that we, being dead to sins, should live unto righteousness: by whose stripes ye were healed."(1 Peter 2:21-24)*

The apostle Peter told us that Jesus Christ knew no sin, yet Moses used a brazen serpent as a symbol of Christ on the cross, healing people.

In the Gospel of St. John Chapter Three, the apostle John also confirms this as he draws reference to Christ fulfilling the event that Moses did in the Old Testament.

God drew my attention to some powerful truths concerning the crucifixion of Jesus Christ.

*"Now from the sixth hour there was darkness over all the land unto the ninth hour: And about the ninth hour Jesus cried with a loud voice, saying, Eli, Eli, lama sabachthani? That is to say, My God, my God, why hast thou forsaken me?" (Matthew 27:45-46)*

This was Jesus' last statement, which is very interesting. This is the first time that Jesus referred to God as "My God." Throughout the Scriptures when ever Jesus referred to God He always addressed Him as 'My Father.' I believe that this was the first time that Jesus was out of the Father's presence.

This was the moment when He fulfilled the serpent lifted up in the wilderness, when He became sin for us, and when He was not allowed into the presence of the Father. Yet, while He was on the cross He was destroying the works of the devil, and healing us by His stripes.

Concerning Jesus Christ statement on the cross, again God spoke another word to me to show me how Holy He is. We believe that Jesus was God manifested in the flesh. We also believe that the fullness of the Godhead was invested in Him.

*"For it pleased the Father that in Him should all fullness dwell." (Colossians 1:19)*
*"For in Him dwelleth all the fullness of the Godhead bodily." (Colossians 2:9)*

I believe that when Jesus made statements, such as **"I and my Father are one,"** recorded in **St. John 10:30**, and *"Verily, verily,*

*I say unto you, The Son can do nothing of Himself, but what He seeth the Father do: for what things so ever He doeth, these also doeth the Son likewise."* Recorded in **St. John 5:19** and His answer to Philip's question in **St. John 14:8-11** when he said *"shew us the Father, and it sufficeth us. Jesus saith unto him, Have I been so long with you, and yet hast thou not known me, Philip?*

*He that hath seen me hath seen the Father; and how sayest thou then shew us the Father? Believest thou not that I am in the Father, and the Father in me?*

*The words that I speak unto you I speak not of myself: but the Father that dwelleth in me, he doeth the works. Believe me that I am in the Father, and the Father in me: or else believe me for the very works' sake."*

Since all of these statements are true concerning Jesus, and He is the only Mediator between God and man, then Jesus was God in the flesh dying on the cross. God said to me that He is so Holy that when He became sin, He could not allow Himself into His own presence.

This is the reason Jesus said, they that worship Him must worship Him in Spirit and in truth and in the beauty of holiness; and holiness without which no man shall see the Lord.

The materials that the people were asked to bring included four different colors of linen: blue, purple, scarlet, and fine linen (white.) These materials were found at the gate of the Tabernacle and they represent the characteristics of Jesus Christ found in the four gospels.

Blue represents the gospel of St. John. John portrays Christ as the Son of God.

*"For God so loved the world that He gave His only begotten Son that whosoever believes in Him shall not perish, but have everlasting life."(St. John 3:16)*

Jesus left Heaven as the Son of God to tell us about the Father, and He left earth as the son of man to tell the Father about us.

The second color is purple which represents royalty, and is portrayed by St. Matthew. The question often asked in Matthew was, is He really the King of the Jews? After the birth of Jesus,

Herod called in the wise men from the East and asked them where was it written that this child would be born that were to be king? This troubled Herod. He sent the wise men to search for the child, and send him word so he also could go and worship Him.

We know that Herod was only concerned about his kingdom and really wanted to have Jesus killed. This was quite evident when he discovered he had been mocked by the wise men that did not return or send him message.

Why would Herod be jealous of a baby? Remember that jealousy involves prophecy. Herod was jealous of Jesus Christ because of the prophecy that Jesus was going to be king.

This story has a message for every person that has a call of God on his or her life. People are jealous of you even though you don't have anything. You may not possess anything now, but evil spirits heard prophecies concerning your future. Know assuredly that the devil is not fighting your present, but your future.

There are many Scriptures in the word of God that points to the birth of Christ. The wise men were able to draw references to the place of Christ birth as was prophesied by Micah the prophet.

*"But thou Bethlehem, Ephratah, though thou be little among the thousands of Judah, yet out of thee shall He come forth unto me that is to be ruler in Israel; whose going forth have been from of old, from everlasting."(Micah 5:2)*

The wise men also referred to the star that was scheduled to appear at the time of the birth of Jesus. They asked, **"Where is He that is born king of the Jews? For we have seen His star in the east and are come to worship Him." (Luke 2:2)**

This prophecy was given by the prophet Balaam, when he was asked by Balak to curse the children of Israel. Balaam's prophecy is recorded in **Numbers 24:17 "I shall see Him, but not now: I shall behold Him, but not nigh: there shall come a Star out of Jacob, and a Sceptre shall rise out of Israel, and shall smite the corners of Moab, and destroy all the children of Sheth."**

The prophet Isaiah told us clearly that Jesus was going to be established upon the throne of His Father David. There are many more prophecies given concerning the Kingship of Jesus Christ. I pointed out that Matthew portrayed Him as the King of Kings.

The next color we will look at is scarlet. Hopefully, we will not spend as much time on this color as we did on the previous ones. However, scarlet represents the suffering savior. This is portrayed by the gospel of **St. Luke.** Even though Luke the beloved physician concentrated his gospel on the healings that were done by Christ, he pointed out to us that this was the reason why he came to suffer and die. Scarlet represents His blood.

In **Joshua 2, w**e see from the story of Rahab the harlot how she hid the two men sent by Joshua to spy out the land. For her kindness, Rahab requested that the lives of her father, mother, sister, brother, and all they had be spared. This request was granted and she used a scarlet cord to pull her family into her house. The scarlet cord was symbolic of the blood of Jesus. On the day that Jericho fell, Rahab and her family were the only ones saved.

The final color at the gate of the Tabernacle was fine linen. Fine linen is white in color and speaks of Christ as the perfect man and perfect God. Both the first and the second Adam had no earthly father.

*"And so it is written, the first man Adam was made a living soul; the last Adam was made a quickening spirit. Howbeit that was not first which is spiritual, but that which is natural; and afterward that which is spiritual. The first man is of the earth, earthly: the second man is of the Lord from Heaven." (1 Corinthians 15:45-47)*

Spices were also used in the Tabernacle. Spices speak of worship. We cannot worship without the Holy Spirit. *"God is a Spirit: and they that worship Him must worship Him in spirit and in truth."* (St. Johns 4:24) The Spirit will not speak of Himself, but whatsoever He shall hear that shall He speak; and He will show you things to come. **"Howbeit when He, the Spirit of Truth, is come, He will guide you into all Truth."(St. John 16:13)**

Sweet Incense represents sweet trials that must bring worship; for the trial of your faith worketh patience.

God switches to the Church when He mentioned Onyx stones. This is symbolic of the Church set in the Ephod and in the breast plate. The Priest represents Jesus Christ; and the stones set in the Ephod represent the Church, the lively stones in Jesus Christ. God always begins from the inside out. He works on our heart first and then the outside.

We will look at the Tabernacle from the outside in. The Gate is called the Way, the door to the Holy Place is called the Truth, and the veil is called the Life.

In **Exodus 25:4-7,** Moses continues to outline the additional materials that God instructed the people to bring. One of these materials was goat hair, which is symbolic of Jesus Christ the Prophet.

Goat hair was used to make ropes. These ropes were used to fasten down each of the sixty poles that supported the Tabernacle. Each pole was capped with silver (Redemption) and the bottom with brass (The suffering Savior.)

The poles were capped with silver, and had silver bolts. Ropes from the top of the pole to bottom were fastened to a brazen nail which was driven halfway into the ground. Nail is a symbol of the death, burial, and resurrection of Jesus Christ. The nail, halfway in the ground, speaks of Jesus being buried in the ground and resurrected in three days. The fastening of the tent using a pole, nail, and rope made of goat's hair, is symbolically a shadow or type of the death, burial, and resurrection of Jesus Christ.

The next material to be used in the tabernacle was Ram's skin dyed red. When ever you see a flock of sheep, the ram is always the leader. This represents Jesus Christ our leader. Dyed red clearly speaks of our leader, who will one day shed His blood.

In **Genesis 22:13,** after Abraham had made up his mind to obey God and had tied up his son Isaac, he discovered that a Ram... not a lamb... were caught in the thicket of the bush. This ram was used in the place of Isaac, symbolic of Jesus Christ our leader that would one day die and take our place.

Badger's skin is a piece of material that God told Moses to ask the people to also bring as an offering. A Badger is a marine animal that has a very ugly skin. This is a shadow or a type of the ugliness of sin that Jesus was going to become for us.

The prophet Isaiah once again tried to describe what Jesus Christ would look like when he faces death on the cross.

*"For He shall grow up before Him as a tender plant, and as a root out of a dry ground: He hath no form nor comeliness; and when we shall see Him, there is no beauty that we should desire Him." (Isaiah 53:2)*

What Isaiah said is that the ugliness of our sins was going to rest upon Jesus and He would have no magnificence, splendor, glory, or honor during His crucifixion.

It is very important to note that even though in certain places of the Bible the angels are referred to as the sons of God, yet they do not know God as Father.

*"And it came to pass, when men began to multiply on the face of the earth, and daughters were born unto them. That the sons of God saw the daughters of men that they were fair; and they took them wives of all which they chose." (Genesis 6:1-2)*

These were fallen angels that the apostle Peter referred to in **1 Peter 3:19, 2 Peter 2:4,** and **Jude 6:7.** The term 'sons of God' as mentioned in Job 1:6, *"Now there was a day when the sons of God came to present themselves before the Lord, and Satan came also among them"* is again mentioned when God answered Job out of a whirlwind and questioned him about the creation and dedication service of this earth.

As God was describing what happened at this event, one of the statement He made is found in **Job 38:7** *"When the morning stars sang together and all the sons of God shouted for joy?"*

When we read Genesis Chapter One, the very first verse stated, **"In the beginning God."** Throughout this entire chapter we read, **"And God."** This continues to the thirty-first verse which is the end of chapter one. This is because in chapter one God is referring to angels, who only know Him as God.

In Genesis Two, God is addressed as The Lord God. In Genesis one there were the Elohim (Trinity) and the angels. At the close of this chapter man was created, and in the second chapter God was demonstrating a relationship that He had with man and not with angels.

As we revisit Jesus on the cross, we must remember this was the first time that Jesus was separated from His Father. Also, this was the first time that God had ever turned His back on His Son. This is the time when He that had no sin became sin for us.

God spoke a word to me concerning this incident on the cross. He said to me that people try to come into His presence any way they want, and with many different unholy things in them. He said, if He did not allow Himself into His own presence when He became sin for us; neither would He allow His people into His presence with sin in their lives.

In **Exodus 25:5,** Moses was also instructed to ask the congregation of Israel to bring a certain kind of wood called Shittim. Wood in the Bible speaks of humanity. However, this wood comes from the acacia tree and is found in Egypt and the Sinai Peninsula in the Middle East.

The acacia tree is a thorn tree and is known for its beauty and durability. It is a wood that needs no special treatment to maintain its long life. It does not rot or decay, and termites cannot eat it. This represents the body of Christ.

*"Now upon the first day of the week, very early in the morning, they came unto the sepulcher, bringing the spices which they had prepared, and certain others with them."*
*(Luke 24:1)*

These followers of Christ were bringing spices to preserve the body of Jesus, even though He told them that He was going to lay His life down and on the third day He will rise again. His followers were confused, disappointed, and didn't clearly understand what He was saying or who He really was. This is the reason why they brought spices. They were going to embalm His body to keep it for a long time.

Today, I am glad that I know something that they didn't know then. The first Adam came from the dust so he had to return to the dust to fulfill the law. The second Adam did not come from the dust. The Word was made flesh and dwell among men. Dust will see corruption, but not the Word.

We said earlier in **Psalms 16:10,** King David through the Holy Spirit saw the incorruptible body of Jesus. He said, *"For thou wilt not leave my soul in hell; neither wilt thou suffer thine Holy One to see corruption."*

King David is dead and buried and his body went back to the dust. We believe that he was waiting for the manifestation of the Lamb who was slain from the foundation of the world. He also made up the first fruit offering when the tombs in Jerusalem burst open during the resurrection of Christ.

I am so glad that Jesus Christ arose from the dead. If He had not risen, there would not have been any hope for me or the millions whose faith in everlasting life is staked on being like Him.

I now have His Spirit, and am striving everyday to be more like Him. One of these days, I will have that same incorruptible body. Praise God for this hope. This gives us great comfort to know that Jesus Christ has become the first fruit of them that slept.

As we continue with the materials used in the tabernacle that they all represent Jesus Christ, we want to look at **Exodus 25:6,** *"Oil for the light, spices for the anointing oil, and for sweet* **incense."**

When we see oil in the Bible, it is symbolic of the anointing. We all know that the word 'Christ' means *"The Anointed One."*

In **Matthew 1:25,** we were told that Joseph knew not Mary until she brought forth her first born son and they called his name Jesus.

Jesus was the only name given by the angels. In **Matthew Chapter 16** when Jesus asked his disciples *"Whom do men say that I the Son of man am",* the disciples responded: "some say thou art John the Baptist, some Elijah, some Jeremiah, and some one of the prophets." Peter, through the inspiration of the Holy Spirit, spoke for the first time the name of the Anointed one.

*"Thou art the Christ, the son of the living God."* This was only known by the Holy Spirit. So Jesus said," *Flesh and blood did not reveal this to you, but my father which is in Heaven."(Matthew 16:17)*

In the tabernacle oil was used for the menorah, or the seven golden candlesticks. The seven golden candlesticks that gave light in the Holy Place were lit by the priest. This represents Jesus the light of the world.

Light represents illumination; light or illumination is revelation of the word. An example: as you receive light or illumination, the same word you read yesterday will become much clearer today.

Jesus had just finished forty days of fasting, and was baptized by the prophet John the Baptist, when He was led by the Holy Spirit into the wilderness to be tempted by the devil.

Jesus, at this time was hungry and satan knew this, so he asked Him to prove that He was the Son of God by turning stones into bread. **Matthew 4:4** states *"But He answered and said, It is written, Man shall not live by bread alone, but by every word that proceedeth out of the mouth of God."*

We have no new Bible and we have no new word, but we have new light. This is the word that is proceeding out of the mouth of God. This is fresh oil. This is one of the reasons that Jesus said Heaven and Earth shall pass away, but the word of God shall last forever.

# CHAPTER THREE

# THE BLOOD OF JESUS CLEANSES THE LEPERS

Whenever a person receives Christ into his or her life they receives some anointing, but this is just the beginning. In the fourteenth chapter of Leviticus, we see a ceremonial cleansing of a leper. The priest had to go out of the camp and sprinkle the leper seven times. Immediately after the cleansing of the leper by blood, the priest was asked to take a log of oil to anoint the leper.

> *"And on the eighth day he shall take two he lambs without blemish, and one ewe lamb of the first year without blemish, and three tenth deals of fine flour for a meat offering, mingled with oil, and one log of oil." (Leviticus 14:10)*

Since we are discussing the blood, I found that the oil which is symbolic of the anointing is never received without the application of the blood.

Let us go into the story of cleansing of the leper a little deeper and see how this story represents the death, burial, and resurrection of Jesus Christ. If Christ didn't go through this process, there would not have been any lepers cleansed or anyone anointed.

In **Leviticus 14**, God spoke unto Moses and told him what the law of cleansing of the leper was going to be. We have been on this little three letter word *"Oil"* for some time, but what I am about to discuss will once again strengthen my case concerning the power in the blood of Jesus.

We are aware of the treatment of persons that became lepers in the Bible. We also know that leprosy represents sin. You may or may not know of the three types of anointing. They are **(1) The Leprous Anointing, (2) The Priestly Anointing, and (3) The Kingly Anointing**. When a person receives salvation in the name of Jesus, immediately he or she receives the first level of anointing called the leprous anointing.

When a person becomes a leper he or she is pronounced unclean by the priest, and is placed or driven outside the camp. Leprosy is a contagious disease and a leper was not allowed to be among the people. This is the reason the priest had to go outside of the camp to cleanse the leper.

> **"And** *the Lord spoke unto Moses, saying, this shall be the law of the leper in the day of his cleansing; He shall be brought unto the priest:*
>
> *And the priest shall go forth out of the camp; and the priest shall look, and behold, if the plague of the leprosy be healed in the leper; Then shall the priest command to take for him that is to be cleansed two birds alive and clean, and cedar wood, and scarlet, and hyssop: And the priest shall command that one of the birds be killed in an earthen vessel over running water: As for the living bird, he shall take it, and the cedar wood, and the scarlet, and the hyssop, and shall dip them and the living bird in the blood of the bird that was killed over the running water:*
>
> *And he shall sprinkle upon him that is to be cleansed from the leprosy seven times, and shall* **pronounce him clean, and shall let the living bird loose into the open field."** *(Leviticus 14:1-7)*

This ceremony continues with the cleansed leper washing his clothes, shaving the hair from his head, beard, eyebrows, and washing his entire body with water. Afterwards, he would take a sin offering to the priest who will offer it unto the Lord on the leper's behalf. Everything that took place in this story points to the coming of Jesus Christ, His death, burial and resurrection.

In the ceremony of cleansing the leper, the first thing that we want to examine is the leper and his separation from the camp. The leper is symbolic of mankind.

When we sinned, we were separated from God's presence. We were driven from His presence and were not allowed back into the camp. The camp represents Heaven. We cannot get to Heaven in our sins, so God sent Jesus (The Priest) who had to leave Heaven (The Camp) and come to earth (Outside the Camp) to redeem mankind back to Him.

Only the priest could cleanse the leper, declare him clean, and bring him back to the camp; and this could only be done by blood.

It is the same with Jesus, and it makes me want to praise His Wonderful Name. Only Jesus can cleanse us with his own blood. Only Jesus can declare that we are clean after His blood has washed away our sins. Jesus Christ is the only one that was able to take the first fruits to Heaven (The Camp).

Jesus will come back to take those who died in Him after His resurrection, and those who are alive and remain: watching and faithful to Heaven (The Camp).This is known as the Rapture of the Church. This is a blessed hope and I feel it is not far away. Praise God for all those He finds watching.

Let us return to the story of the cleansing of the leper. The priest was instructed by Moses who, I must remind you, was instructed by God to take two living birds. The birds were to be from the species of birds listed as clean, and were to be accompanied by cedar wood, scarlet, and hyssop. One of the birds was to be killed in an earthen vessel over running water. The killing of this bird represents Jesus Christ dying in a fleshly (Earthen) body. Dipping the second bird in the blood of the dead bird and sprinkling the leper seven times, is a symbol of Jesus Christ shedding His blood on seven occasions during His crucifixion.

The first time Jesus shed his blood was while He prayed in the garden of Gethsemane. His sweat became as drops of blood. The second time was when He was before Pilate and he had Him scourged. The third time came shortly after this scourging; they plaited a crown of thorns and placed it on His head, and mocked Him. The fourth and fifth times were the piercing of His hands. The nailing of His feet was the sixth time and the seventh was the piercing of His side.

The freedom of the living bird flying away into the Heavens is a foreshadow of the resurrection and ascension of Jesus Christ. Please do not forget that if you want to really get a better understanding of God's word, whenever you read or study His word, look for Jesus. Everything that God ever planned is manifested in Jesus.

## FIRST OIL

After the leper had been cleansed, the priest was instructed to slay the lamb brought for sacrifice, in the Holy Place where he normally would kill the sin offering and burnt offering.

*"And the priest shall take some of the blood of the trespass offering, and the priest shall put it upon the tip of the right ear of him that is to be cleansed, and upon the thumb of his right hand, and upon the great toe of the right foot: And the Priest shall take some of the log of oil, and pour it into the palm of his own left hand: and the priest shall dip his right finger in the oil that is in his left hand, and shall sprinkle of the oil with his finger seven times before the LORD. And of the rest of the oil that is in his hand shall the priest put upon the tip of the right ear of him that is to be cleansed, and upon the thumb of his right hand, and upon the great toe of his right foot, upon the blood of the trespass offering: And the remnant of the oil that is in the priest's hand he shall pour upon the head of him that is to be cleansed: And the priest shall make an atonement for him before the LORD." (Leviticus 14:14-18)*

I have taken time and space to stress to you that no one can receive an anointing unless they come through the blood of Jesus. We may have titles and credentials behind our names, but the anointing on our life came only because of the blood of Jesus Christ.

# A SPECIAL KIND OF OIL

Have you notice that in **Exodus 25:6** there were spices for the anointing oil? This oil was going to be different and was going to have different uses. The oil had special spices added to it and would be used for two special purposes: (1) to anoint the furniture in the tabernacle, and (2) to anoint Aaron and his sons for the service of priest, who will minister in the tabernacle.

This is one of the major reasons why you should not just place yourself in a ministry office just because you feel you should hold a certain position. You can call yourself by a certain name, and be held in high standing in the community where you live, but can you anoint yourself for the name you are calling yourself?

*"Moreover the Lord spake unto Moses, saying, Take thou unto thee principal spices, of pure myrrh five hundred shekels, and of sweet cinnamon half so much, even two hundred and fifty shekels, and of sweet calamus two hundred and fifty shekels; and of cassia five hundred shekels after the shekels of the sanctuary, and of oil olive an hin: And thou shall make an oil of holy ointment, an ointment compound after the art of the apothecary: It shall be a holy anointing oil.*

*And thou shall anoint the tabernacle of the congregation therewith, and the ark of the testimony, and the table and all its vessels, and the candlestick and his vessel, and the altar of incense. And the altar of burnt offering with all his vessels, and the laver and its foot. And thou shall sanctify them, that they may be most holy: Whatsoever touch them shall be holy. And thou shall anoint Aaron and his sons, and consecrate them, that they may minister unto me in the priest's office.*

*And thou shall speak unto the children of Israel, saying, this shall be an holy anointing oil unto me throughout your generations. Upon man's flesh shall it not be poured, neither shall ye make any like it, after the composition of it: It is holy, and it shall be holy unto you. Whosoever compoundeth any like it, or whosoever putteth any of it upon a stranger, shall even be cut off from his people." (Exodus 30:22-33)*

I would like to explain in more details every small item mentioned in these passages, but because of the subject matter of this book, I will explain sufficient to support the awesome power that is in the blood of Jesus.

God also told Moses that in addition to the spices for the anointing oil, there must be spices for incense. The altar of incense sits just in front of the veil of the temple. Incense speaks of the trials that a person must go through.

In **Exodus 25:6**, the Bible refers to this incense as sweet incense. People never call their trials sweet, especially when they are going through them. It is just as the apostle Paul said in *2 Corinthians 4:17, "For our light affliction, which is but for a moment, worketh for us a far more exceeding and eternal weight of glory."*

If while reading this book you have not read the life story of the apostle Paul, I suggest that you take some time and do so. Please pay special attention to the number of tough trials Paul went through, and still was able to call them 'light afflictions.' This was simply because of God, and that he clearly understood the purpose of these trials.

As we return to the materials for the tabernacle, we notice that God requested spices for the incense. Incense is never one substance, but many substances compounded. Each of these spices represents a trial that we have to go through before we get behind the veil.

Please remember that you have to burn the incense, and the smoke must go before you into the Holy of Holies. To burn your trials you must worship God. Remember that no one is allowed into the presence of God without worship, or without the blood. From the altar of sacrifice in the outer court, to the Holy of Holies there is a labor of love. No matter how the priest labored he could not enter into the Holy of Holies unless he takes the blood with him.

I want to draw your attention to the word *"Trials."* This word causes many to just quit on God. When ever I am faced with trials, I would always go to my favorite Scripture which gives me strength to make it. For many years God has allowed the Holy Sprit to minister a word to my spirit that has helped me through my Christian walk. I do not believe there are any trials that God permits us to go through that was sent to kill us. I believe there are a perfect will and a permissive will of God in people's lives. I believe that the perfect will of God is to heal every person, and to bring everyone through their trials so the glory would come to His name.

*"We then, as workers together with Him, beseech you also that ye receive not the grace of God in vain." (2 Corinthians 6:1)*

From verses four through ten of 2 Corinthians 6, there are a number of trials that a believer will go through. Here the apostle Paul tells us that for every one of these trials, God has given us a measure of grace. He also started out by telling us that if we do not utilize the grace that we have received for these trials, then we have received the grace of God in vain.

If you can get the revelation of what Paul said in **2 Corinthians 12:9** *"My grace is sufficient for thee: for my strength is made perfect in weakness,"* you can become resolved and know that your battle is not with flesh and blood; then no matter what trials come your way, you will overcome.

## THE HIGH PRIEST COVERING

Again, I want to remind you that the whole tabernacle in the wilderness was Jesus Christ. As we continue, let us look at the additional materials found in **Exodus 25:7:** *"Onyx stones, and stones to be set in the ephod, and in the breastplate."* The first mention of onyx stone is found in the book of Genesis. When God was describing the water system that He placed in the Garden of Eden, one of the precious gems mentioned was onyx stones.

*"And a river went out of Eden to water the garden; and from thence it was parted, and became into four heads. The name of the first one is Pison: that is which compasseth the*

*whole land of Havilah, where there is gold; And the gold of that land is good: there is bdellium and the onyx stone."* *(Genesis 2:10-12)*

Onyx stones are a gem of a pale green color. Two of these were engraved with the names of the twelve tribes of Israel. Six names were engraved in each stone. These stones were placed in the ephod or the shoulder of the priest's garment. In addition, twelve stones with the names of the twelve tribes of Israel engraved in them were placed in the breastplate.

*"And they shall take gold, and blue and purple, and scarlet and fine linen.*

*And they shall make the ephod of gold, of blue, and of purple, of scarlet, and fine twined linen, with cunning work. It shall have two shoulder pieces thereof joined at the two edges thereof; and so shall it be joined together. And the curious girdle of the ephod, which is upon it, shall be of the same, according to the work thereof; even of gold, of blue, and purple, and scarlet, and fine twined linen.*

*And thou shalt take two onyx stones, and grave on them the names of the children of Israel: Six of their names on one stone, and the other six names of the rest on the other stone, according to their birth. With the work of an engraver in stone, like the engravings of a signet, shalt thou engrave the two stones with the names of the children of Israel: thou shalt make them to be set in ouches of gold.*

*And thou shall put the two stones upon the shoulders of the ephod for stones of memorial unto the children of Israel: And Aaron shall bear their names before the Lord upon his two shoulders for a memorial. And thou shalt make ounces of gold; and two chains of pure gold at the ends; of wreathen work shalt thou make them, and fasten the wreathen chain to the ouches." (Exodus 28:5-14)*

It is very important to note that twelve precious stones were also used in the breastplate of the priest robe. Each stone represents one of the sons of the tribes of Israel. These were arranged in four rows, and in sets of threes.

The following is a list and the order of arrangements of the precious stones that were on the priest robe as recorded in **Exodus 28: 17-21.**

**First Row** (Exodus 28:17)

**Sardius - Reuben** (Genesis 29:32): A beautiful gem of blood red color.

**Topaz - Simeon** (Genesis 29:33): A pale green stone with mixture of yellow.

**Carbuncle - Levi** (Genesis 29:34): A gem of deep red color with a mixture of scarlet.

**Second Row** (Exodus 28:18)

**Emerald - Judah** (Genesis 29:35): A bright red green color without any other mixture.

**Sapphire - Dan** (Genesis 30:6): A gem of clear blue color and next in hardness to the diamond.

**Diamond - Naphtali** (Genesis 30:8): A clear, sparkling gem of great value.

**Third Row** (Exodus 28:19)

**Ligure - Gad** (Genesis 30:11): The same as the jacinth stone of dull red or cinnamon color with a mixture of yellow.

**Agate - Asher** (Genesis 30:13): A white, reddish yellowish and greenish stone of the flint family and the cheapest of all precious stones.

**Amethyst - Issachar** (Genesis 30:18): A gem with deep red and strong blue colors which give it a purple hue.

**Fourth Row** (Exodus 28:20)

**Beryl - Zebulun** (Genesis 30:20): A stone of bluish green color. Some think the chrysolite is meant here. If so, it would be a gem of yellowish green color.

**Onyx - Joseph** (Genesis 30:24): A stone of various colors- One consisting of layers of different colors.

**Jasper - Benjamin** (Genesis 35:16-19): A gem of bright green color sometimes clouded with white and spotted with red and yellow. Mineralogists list 15 varieties of jasper: green, red, yellow, brown, violet, black, bluish gray, milky white, and various combinations of colors.

I want you to notice, that the covering that was on lucifer had the same precious stones.

According to **Ezekiel 28:11-13,** God gave the prophet Ezekiel a glimpse of lucifer's covering when he was in Eden, the garden of God. *"Moreover the word of the Lord came onto me, saying, Son of man take up a lamentation upon the king of Tyrus, and say unto him, thus said the Lord God, thou sealest up the sun, full of wisdom, and perfect in beauty. Thou has been in Eden the garden of God, every precious stone as thy covering, the sardius, topaz, and the diamond, the beryl, the onyx, and the jasper, the sapphire, the emerald, and the carbuncle, and gold: The workmanship of thy tabrets and of thy pipes was prepared in thee in the day that thou wast created." (Ezekiel 28: 11-13)*

This is one of the most interesting comparisons in the Bible. lucifer's covering had the same precious stones as those of the High Priest. However, lucifer's covering was missing the third row of stones. Three is God's number of perfection, and if you examine the precious stones that were in the third row you would notice that they were reserved for the High Priest of Heaven, who is Jesus Christ.

The third row of precious stones that were on the High Priest's robe, and missing from lucifer's covering were (1) Ligure - Gad, (2) Agate - Asher, and (3) Amethyst - Issachar.

This may seem unimportant to you at this time, but for you to get the wisdom behind the leaving out of these stones from lucifer's covering, you have to take a look at Genesis 49 where Jacob called his sons and prophesied to each of them. He told them who they were then, but he also told them what their future was going to be.

This is what makes the High Priest's robe so very important; whoever the sons of Jacob were and whatever their future held, was resting on and taken into the Holiest of Holy on the priest's robe.

*"And Jacob called unto his sons, and said; gather your-selves together, that I may tell you that which shall befall you in the last days. Gather yourselves together, and hear,*

*ye sons of Jacob; and hearken unto Israel your father."*
*(Genesis 49:1-2)*

From here, Jacob started with his eldest son Reuben and ended with his last son Benjamin.

Let us now look at the three sons that were in the third row of the priest robe, and missing from lucifer's covering. **"Gad** *a troop shall overcome him, but he shall overcome at last."(Genesis 49:19)*

The stone ligure, representing Gad, was missing from lucifer's covering because he was already defeated, and will never overcome; neither will he help anyone to overcome. Overcoming is left solely for the High Priest in Heaven, who is Jesus Christ.

*"Out of Asher, his bread shall be fat, and he shall yield royal daintie."(Genesis 49:20)*

This son represented as the precious stone Agate, was missing from lucifer's covering because satan was never royal and never will be. Royalty is reserved for the one and only Saviour of this world and His name is Jesus. The next son Issachar, is represented by the precious stone Amethyst. This stone was in the third row and was missing from lucifer's covering. Jacob prophesied to him:

*"Issachar is a strong ass couching down between two burdens: And he saw that rest was good and the land that it was pleasant: And bowed his shoulder to bear: and became a servant unto tribute." (Genesis 49:14-15)*

This passage speaks of a burden and rest; none of these are attributes of satan. He will never be a burden bearer, and he will never help anyone to find rest. We now understand why lucifer thought he was important and allowed pride to get into his heart.

God has reserved overcoming, royalty, and burden bearing for Jesus Christ alone. Praise God! He has always reserved all power and total control to Himself, and has demonstrated and revealed this Power in His Son Jesus Christ, the Last High Priest. Jesus is the Sacrificial Lamb, who took His own blood into Heaven and sprinkled the furniture in the Heavenly Tabernacle. There is no more need for another sacrifice.

This is much more than lucifer can say. There is no record of him shedding blood for anyone; after all, lucifer is just a fallen angel and angels have no blood.

This is why in satanic rituals they are always looking for humans or animals to sacrifice to the devil. You will never see satan shed his blood for any one, simply because he has no blood.

*"Yet Michael the archangel, when contending with the devil he disputed about the body of Moses, durst not bring against him a railing accusation, but said, the Lord rebuke thee." (Jude 9)*

Before Jesus Christ died, satan had the legal rights or the power over death.

*"Blotting out the handwriting of ordinances that was against us, which was contrary to us, and took it out of the way, nailing them to the cross; And having spoil principalities and powers, He made a show of them in it openly triumphing over them in it." (Colossian 2:14-15)*

The apostle Paul got a revelation of this victory over death that was accomplished by Jesus Christ on the cross.

*"Forasmuch then as the children are partakers of the flesh and blood, he also Himself likewise took part of the same; that through death He might destroy Him, that had the power of death, that is the devil. And deliver them who through fear of death were all their lifetime subject to bondage." (Hebrews 2:14-15)*

While the apostle John was on the Isle of Patmos, he got one of the greatest revelations from Jesus Christ. It is very important to point out to the reader that this was Jesus after His resurrection. He was revealing Himself and the things that would take place at the conclusion of man's week of redemption to John.

In **Revelation 1:18**, Jesus said, *"I am He that liveth, and was dead; and behold, I am alive for evermore, Amen; and have the keys of Hell and death."*

## YOUR ANGELS NEED YOUR ASSISTANCE

There is no victory or overcoming without the blood of Jesus. This is one of the reasons I feel that the blood of Jesus is taken too lightly today. Even though Michael was an archangel, he needed the blood of Jesus to rebuke the devil. In Revelation there is a war described in Heaven.

> *"And there was war in Heaven: Michael and his angels fought against the dragon; and the dragon fought and his angels,*
> *And prevail not; neither was their place found any more in Heaven.*
> *And the great dragon was cast out, that which decieveth the whole world: he was cast out into the earth, and his angels were cast out with him.*
> *And I heard a loud voice saying in Heaven, Now is come salvation, and strength, and the kingdom of our God, and the power of His Christ: for the accuser of our brethren is cast down, which accused them before our God day and night. And they overcame him by the blood of the lamb, and by the word of their testimony; and they loved not their lives unto the death."* (Revelation 12: 7-11)

The subject of angels and the blood is a study in itself that we will not get into detail in this book. However, I want you to understand the role that angels play in our daily lives.

> *"But to which of the angels said He at any time, Sit on my right hand, until I make thine enemies thy footstool? Are they not all ministering spirits, sent forth to minister for them who shall be heirs of salvation?"* (Hebrews 1:13-14)

Allow me to say, all the angels that are sent to minister for us according to **Hebrews 1:13-14,** are depending on us to help them win our battles that are being fought in the heavenlies. This can only be done by praying the word of God, and pleading the blood of Jesus Christ.

**Psalms 103:20** states, **"Bless the Lord, ye His angels that excel in strength, that do His** *commandments, hearkening onto the voice of His word."*

Please don't forget, praying the word will cause our angel to do what the word said; and pleading the blood of Jesus Christ will cause them to get stronger.

# CHAPTER FOUR

# FINISHED AT THE BEGINNING

The pattern of the tabernacle was not Moses' idea. It was a pattern made after the likeness of an original one in Heaven. The priest's robe was a replica of Jesus Christ our High Priest in Heaven.

I believe that Jesus Christ existed long before God gave Moses the instructions and revelation of His word to start writing the Bible.

As you read this book, always keep in mind that these symbols are shadows used in the Old Testament that follows the original furniture in heaven. Each piece of furniture in the tabernacle was positioned in the exact way as Jesus hung on the cross.

All of the materials in the tabernacle speak of some area of Jesus' life and ministry.

The Brazen Altar of sacrifice represents the piercing of Jesus feet. The Laver represents the piercing of His side. The lamp stand, the Menorah or seven candlesticks, was a picture of the out-stretched right hand of Jesus. To the opposite side of the candlestick was the Table of Shewbread representing Jesus' out-stretched left hand.

The Golden Altar of incense is a symbol of His bowels that turned within Him. The Veil represented His flesh that was torn for us. The Ark of the Covenant represents the crown of thorns that was placed upon His head.

As I mentioned before, these materials were shadows and shadows need objects. Object needs some light to shine on it so that the shadows can be seen. The shadow from the cross came from the fourth day of God's week of man's redemption. In other words, Jesus Christ was crucified on the fourth day of God's week of man's redemption.

God does not live in time; God lives outside of time. God created time and time lives in Him. God does not have a future, God holds the future. Everything in God is eternal, and God lives in eternity and eternity lives in Him.

*"Forever O Lord, Thy word is settled in Heaven."(Psalms 119:89)*

This verse of Scripture tells us that long before man was created, God's word was settled in Heaven. In Genesis One, God came and restored the earth. He used one week to complete the restoration of the earth.

Using the **'like as principal'** one day with God is as a thousand years; God gave us one week or seven days to complete his eternal purpose in man.

> *"But beloved be not ignorant of this one thing, that one day is with the Lord as a thousand years, and a thousand years as one day." (2 Peter 3:8)*
> *"For a thousand years in thy sight are as yesterday when it is past, and as a watch in the night."(Psalms 90:4)*

The above Scripture shows the origin of this statement: that on the fourth day Jesus Christ was crucified, and the light from the seventh day shone on the cross in the fourth day and cast a shadow in the Old Testament.

Jesus said that we are the light of the world, and it was prophesied by King David that out of Zion the perfection of beauty God hath shined. This can be further clarified in **Psalms 50:1-2.**

> *"The mighty God, even the Lord hath spoken, and called the earth from the rising of the sun unto the going down*

*thereof. Out of Zion, the perfection of beauty, God hath shined." (Psalms 50:1-2)*

This is a prophecy of the light that God sees shining from a perfect church in the third dimension on the seventh day. This light shone on Jesus while He was on the cross in the fourth day of man's prophetic week.

Jesus on the cross is the object in the fourth day of man's prophetic week. The light from the perfect church in the seventh day shone on Jesus, and cast a shadow of the tabernacle that Moses built.

The fifth day is the first thousand years after the resurrection of Jesus Christ. Five in God is the number for grace, thus we have the first day or the first dimension of grace.

In the year 2000 AD, we completed the second thousand or the second day of grace. Now that we are presently in the seventh millennium, it is obvious that we have entered a new day. A new one thousand years, this is a new millennium.

This day is the seventh day of man's prophetic week, and the third day after the resurrection of Jesus Christ. This day is also the third dimension of Grace.

The church of the Lord Jesus Christ should be enjoying complete rest and perfection.

Have you noticed how God in His infinite wisdom allowed the seventh day of man's week, and the third day after the resurrection of Jesus Christ to culminate into the same day? This day is called the Lord's Day.

*"I John who also am your brother, and companion in tribulation, and in the kingdom and patience of Jesus Christ, was in the Isles that is called Patmos, for the word of God, and for the testimony of Jesus Christ. I was in the Spirit on the Lord's Day, and heard behind me a great voice, as of a trumpet." (Revelation 1:9-10)*

Here the apostle John in the Spirit, transcended time. In the fifth day John was in person, but in the seventh day he was in the Spirit.

Jesus Christ gave John a revelation of what condition the churches and the pastors would be in during the seventh day of man's week, or the third day after the resurrection of Jesus Christ.

The seventh day represents *the rest of God*, and the third day represents *perfection*. This is the day when the church will be perfected and come to a place of rest. However, this can only be done when the church goes back to the cross and go through the death, burial, and resurrection process.

Only resurrected saints can flow with what God is doing today in the third dimension, because in the first dimension is all man. In the second dimension is man and God, but in the third dimension it is all God. Since only resurrected saints are going to be able to flow in this third dimension, now I can clearly understand why the apostle Paul said that only some are going to enter therein.

> *"Let us therefore fear, lest, a* **promise** *being left us of entering into His rest, any of you should seem to come short of it.*
>
> *For unto us was the gospel preached, as well as unto them: but the word preached did not profit them, not being mixed with faith in them that heard it.*
>
> *For we which have believed do enter into rest, as He said, as I have sworn in my wrath, if they shall enter into my rest: although the works were finished from the foundation of the world.*
>
> *For He spake in a certain place of the seventh day on this wise, and God did rest the seventh day from all His works.*
>
> *And in this place again, If they shall enter into my rest. Seeing therefore it remaineth that some must enter therein, and they to whom it was first preached entered not in because of unbelief;*
>
> *Again, He limiteth a certain day, saying in David, Today after so long a time; as it is said, to day if ye will hear His voice, harden not your hearts.*
>
> *For if Jesus had given them rest, then would He not afterward have spoken of another day.*

*There remaineth therefore a rest to the people of God.*

*For He that is entered into His rest, He also hath ceased from His own works, as God did from His. Let us labor therefore to enter into that rest, lest any man fall after the same example of unbelief." (Hebrews 4:1-11)*

**Hebrews 4:12** tells us,

*"The word of God is quick and powerful and sharper than any two edged sword, piercing even to the dividing asunder of the soul and spirit, and of the joints and marrow, and is a discerner of the thoughts and intents of the heart."*

Here we are told that the word of God would cut through the third dimension. From this scripture, we can see that those who will enter into rest are those persons who have died to self. Those who know that the glory belongs to God for every thing that He does through His vessels.

Let us return to the priest and the Tabernacle. Onyx stones that were placed on the shoulder of the priest's garment had six of the leaders of the tribe of Israel engraved in each of them. The breast plate had the twelve stones with the names of the twelve tribes of the Children of Israel engraved in them.

Aaron and his sons were consecrated to minister daily to God in the priest's office. They would sacrifice animals every day, but Aaron the high priest would make atonement for the sins of the people once a year.

Let us take a look at the preparation for this atonement.

*"And thou shalt make an altar to burn incense upon: of shittim wood shalt thou make it. A cubit shalt be the length thereof, and a cubit the breath thereof; foursquare shall it be: and two cubits shall be the height thereof: the horns thereof shall be of the same.*

*And thou shall overlay it with pure gold, the top thereof and the sides thereof round about, and the horns thereof; and thou shall make unto it a crown of gold round about.*

> *And two golden rings shalt thou make to it under the crown of it, by the two corners thereof, upon the two sides of it shalt thou make it; and they shall be for places for the staves to bear it withal.*
>
> *And thou shall make the staves of shittim wood, and overlay them with gold.*
>
> *And thou shall put it before the veil that is before the ark of the testimony, before the mercy seat that is over the testimony, where I will meet with thee.*
>
> *And Aaron shall burn thereon sweet incense every morning: When he dresseth the lamps, he shall burn incense upon it. And when Aaron lighteth the lamps at even, he shall burn incense upon it, a perpetual incense before the Lord throughout your generations. Ye shall offer no strange incense thereon, nor burnt sacrifice, nor meat offering; neither shall ye pour drink offering thereon. And Aaron shall make an atonement upon the horn of it once in a year with the blood of the sin offering of atonement: Once in the year shall he make atonement upon it throughout your generations: It is most holy unto the Lord." (Exodus 30: 1-10)*

This is one of the most powerful foreshadowing of the complete work of Jesus Christ on the cross. Remember that the high priest represents The High Priest in Heaven, who is Jesus Christ.

Aaron, the high priest, had to kill a lamb and offer the lamb's blood for the people's sin, but Jesus Christ was both lamb and priest.

John while baptizing in the river Jordan saw Jesus coming and said in **St. John 1:29, "Behold the Lamb of God which taketh away the sin of** *the world."* John assured us that this was the one who was going to baptize with the Holy Ghost and with fire. God told him that the one, whom he sees the Holy Spirit descending like a dove and remaining on, was the one he came to prepare the way for, and was going to baptize with the Holy Ghost and Fire. John also declared that this Jesus was going to have the Spirit without measure.

# THE ETERNAL PRIESTLINE

While John introduced us to Lamb, the apostle Paul exposed us to the Last High Priest.

*"But Christ being come an High Priest of good things to come by a greater and more perfect tabernacle, not made with hands, that is to say, not of this building; Neither by the blood of goats and calves, but by His own blood He entered in once into the Holy Place, having obtained eternal redemption for us."(Hebrews 9:11-12)*

It is true that Jesus is the last High Priest. However, He did not come through the Aaronic or the Levitical priest line. Before there was the Aaronic or the Levitical priest line, Jesus had established His own Priest Line. Jesus came through the Melchizedek order.

*"The Lord hath sworn, and will not repent, thou art a Priest for ever* **after the order of Melchizedek."** *(Psalms 110:4)*

We will examine the Melchizedek order a little closer.

*"And Melchizedek king of Salem brought forth bread and wine: and he was the Priest of the Most High God.*

*And he blessed him, and said, blessed be* **Abram** *of the Most High God, possessor of Heaven and Earth:*

*And blessed be the Most High God, which hath delivered thine enemies into thy hand. And he gave Him tithes of all."(Genesis 14:18-20)*

Here Abram gave tithes to the king, and the king gave Abram bread and wine. This king must have known something for he gave Abram the elements that are used in the Lord's Supper. The bread represented Jesus' body and the wine His blood. Abram did not know this at that time, but today we can see it much clearer than yesterday. Everything that was done in the Old Testament points to the death, burial, and resurrection of Jesus Christ.

The word Salem is the ancient name for Jerusalem. It is also the Hebrew word for Shalom, which means peace. This means that Abram paid tithes to the first king of Jerusalem, King of peace, who was also the high priest. The apostle Paul called him the king of righteousness.

*"For this Melchizedek, king of Salem, priest of the Most High God, who met Abraham returning from the slaughter of the kings, and blessed him; To whom also Abraham gave a tenth part of all; first being by interpretation king of righteousness, and after that King of Salem, which is king of Peace. Without father, without mother, without descent, having neither beginning of days, nor end of life; But made like unto the Son of God; abideth a priest continually." (Hebrews 7:1-3)*

In **Revelation 1:8,** Jesus told the apostle John that He was the Alpha and the Omega; the beginning and the ending, which Is, and which Was, and which Is to come, the Almighty.

I believe that there is no one else that can fit all the characteristics of Melchizedek like Jesus Christ Himself. He is the First, and will be the last King and Priest of Jerusalem. Likewise, the First and Last Priest and King of Righteousness.

Our Bible clearly shows us that the Aaronic priest line was just a type or a shadow. According to the scriptures, everything that Moses built in the Tabernacle was after a pattern in Heaven, including the high priest garments.

I believe that Jesus came and established His own priest line in the Old Testament, and permitted a temporary priest line through Aaron, or the Levitical Priest Line. He picked up His Priest Line in the New Testament.

God instructed Moses that the priest line was coming from the tribe of Levi, the same tribe that Moses himself came from.

In **Genesis 49,** it is clear that Jesus was going to come through the tribe of Judah. In **verses 9-10** we read,

*"Judah is a lion's whelp: from the prey, my son, thou art gone up: he stooped down, he couched as a lion, and as an old lion; who shall rouse him up?*

*The sceptre shall not depart from Judah, nor a lawgiver from between his feet, until Shiloh come; and unto Him shall the gathering of the people be."*

Judah slept with his daughter-in-law Tamar and she conceived and twins were born. These twins were called Pharez and Zarah.

**Deuteronomy 23:2** states, *"A bastard shall not enter into the congregation of the Lord; even to his tenth generation shall not he not enter into the congregation of the LORD."*

King David was the tenth king from Judah through the linage of Pharez.

*"Now these are the generation of Pharez: Pharez begat Hezron,*

*And Hezron begat Ram, and Ram begat Amminadab,*

*And Amminadab begat Nahshon. And Nahshon begat salmon, And Salmon begat Boaz, And Boaz begat Obed, And Obed begat Jesse, and Jesse begat David." (Ruth 4:18-22)*

Jesus Christ came through the linage of David.

All of this information about the genealogy of Jesus Christ shows us clearly that Jesus did not come through the Levitical priest line.

Over the years we have missed so many hidden truths concerning Jesus in the Old Testament. When John the Baptist saw Jesus and was asking Jesus to baptize him instead, Jesus said unto him, *"Suffer it to be so now: for thus it becometh us to fulfill all righteousness."* *(Matthew 3:15)* The Bible said, and then he suffered Him.

John's father Zechariah was a priest of the course of Abia. His mother Elizabeth was of the daughters of Aaron. Both John's mother and father came through priest lines. By law John was next in line to inherit the priest line. John showed no interest in these priest lines, but baptized the last High Priest

At age 30, all priests were put under water before they could enter the priest line and perform priestly duties.

Jesus Christ came to John and told him suffer it to be so to fulfill all righteousness. This was done when both Jesus and John were 30 years old; John being only six months older. (According to the law for a priest to enter the priest hood, he had to be between the ages of 30 and 50. He also had to be baptized by a high priest that was between the same ages. Since Jesus had not died yet, he had to fulfill the law by being baptized by a high priest.)

When Jesus came out of the water, He reconnected the Melchizedek priest line; the eternal priest line that seemed to have been silent from its introduction in the fourteenth chapter of the book of Genesis. No one else can fit into this Melchizedek order but Jesus Christ and this makes Him the Last High Priest.

# CHAPTER FIVE

# THE FIRST DAY OF PENTECOST

In **Exodus 19**, when the children of Israel had travelled from Egypt, on the first day of the third month they came to the wilderness of Sinai. God told Moses to ask the people to sanctify themselves for three days. These three days made fifty days, and God came down on Mount Sinai.

*"And the LORD said unto Moses, go unto the people, and sanctify them today and tomorrow, and let them wash their clothes, and be ready against the third day: for the third day the LORD will come down in the sight of all the people upon mount Sinai."(Exodus 19:10-11)*

On the fiftieth day the Ten Commandments were given audibly to the children of Israel. This was the first day of Pentecost. This is the reason why in the second chapter of Acts we read, *"And when the day of Pentecost had fully come."*

The word **'fully'** tells us that Pentecost was always there, but it could not fully come until Jesus had come and fulfilled all of the feasts of Israel.

The first day of the third month would make the day of the giving of the law the fiftieth day or the day of Pentecost, after Israel left Egypt on the fifteenth day of the first month.

*"And they departed from Rameses in the first month, on the fifteenth day of the first month; on the morrow after the Passover*

*the children of Israel went out with an high hand in the sight of all the Egyptians."*(**Numbers 33:3**)

The day of Pentecost was after seven Sabbaths (49 days) were completed or the fiftieth day after the Passover.

*"And he shall wave the sheaf before the Lord, to be accepted for you: on the morrow after the Sabbath the priest shall wave it." (Leviticus 23:11)*

*"And ye shall count unto you from the morrow after the Sabbath from the day that you brought the sheaf offering; seven Sabbaths shall be completed: Even unto the morrow after the seventh Sabbath shall ye number fifty days; and ye shall offer a new meat offering unto the Lord." (Leviticus 23:15-16)*

We can now say that beginning with the 16th day of the first month and counting 50 days would mean the law was given on Pentecost as follows. Israel left Egypt the 15th of April and on the Sabbath, as was made clear in **Numbers 33:3**. The 16th was the start of the 50 days to Pentecost. The 16th of the first month, to the 1st day of the third month would be 46 days.

*In the third month, when the children of Israel were gone forth out of the land of Egypt, the same day came they into the wilderness of Sinai." (Exodus 19:1)*

Moses went up into the mount the next day after camping in the mount on the 2nd day of the third month.

*"And Moses went up unto God, and the Lord called unto him out of the mountain, saying, thus shalt thou say to the house of Jacob, and tell the children of Israel; Ye have seen what I did unto the Egyptians, and how I bare you on eagles' wings, and brought you unto myself.*

*Now therefore, if you will obey my voice indeed, and keep my covenant, then ye shall be a peculiar treasure unto me above all people: for all the earth is mine:*

*And ye shall be unto me a kingdom of priest, and an holy nation. These are the words which thou shalt speak unto the children of Israel." (Exodus 19:3-9)*

The plan of God does not change. So we see the fulfillment of this promise in the New Testament as one high priest baptized another.

This High priest that was being baptized was also the King of Kings, thus the apostle Peter called this priest line "A Royal Priesthood."

*"But ye are a chosen generation, a Royal Priesthood, an holy nation, a peculiar people; that ye should shew forth the praises of Him who had called you out of darkness into His marvelous light:*

*Which in time past were not a people, but are now the people of God: which had not obtained mercy, but now have obtained mercy." (1Peter 2:9-10)*

The Israelites was commanded to sanctify themselves for three days. On the third day of Sanctification, God gave them the law. (**Exodus 19:10-15**)

These three days were the third, fourth, and the fifth day of the third month. The forty-sixth day, the first day in the month, and the three days of sanctification makes fifty days. The fiftieth day was the day the law was given or the day of Pentecost.

# A GLIMPSE OF PASSOVER

*"And the Lord spake unto Moses and Aaron in the land of Egypt, saying, this month shall be unto you the beginning of months: It shall be the first month of the year to you.*

*Speak ye unto all the congregation of Israel, saying, in the tenth day of this month they shall take to them every man a lamb, according to the house of their fathers, a lamb for a house:*

*And if the household be too little for the lamb, let him and his neighbor next unto his house take it according to number of the souls; every man according to his eating shall make your count for the lamb.*

*Your lamb shall be without blemish, a male of the first year: ye shall take it out from the sheep, or from the goats:*

*And ye shall keep it up until the fourteenth day of the same month: and the whole assembly of the congregation of Israel shall kill it in the evening.*

*And they shall take of the blood, and strike it on the two side posts and on the upper door post of the houses, wherein they shall eat it.*

*And they shall eat the flesh in that night, roast with fire, and unleavened bread; and with bitter herbs they shall eat it.*

*Eat not it raw, nor sodden at all with water, but roast with fire; his head with his legs, and with the purtenance thereof.*

*And ye shall let nothing of it remain until the morning; and that which remaineth of it until the morning ye shall burn with fire.*

*And thus shall ye eat it; with your loins girded, your shoes on your feet, and your staff in your hand; and ye shall eat it in haste: it is the Lord's Passover.*

*For I will pass through the land of Egypt this night, and will smite all the firstborn in the land of Egypt, both man and beast; and against all the gods of Egypt I will execute judgment: I am the Lord.*

*And the blood shall be to you for a token upon the houses where ye are: and when I see the blood, I will pass over you, and the plague shall not be upon you to destroy you, when I smite the land of Egypt.*

*And this day shall be unto you for a memorial; and ye shall keep it a feast to the Lord throughout your generations; ye shall keep it a feast by an ordinance forever."(Exodus 12:1-14)*

The previous passage of Scripture fulfilled a promise that God made to Abraham. The Children of Israel left Egypt on the four hundred and thirtieth day of the dispensation of promise. The same day to make 430 years, the Lord's Passover was instituted the night before.

Fifty days from Passover, the Children of Israel experienced the first day of Pentecost or the feast of Pentecost. This was a new experience for them and there the law was also given, but they were not ready for this new experience.

## PENTECOST FULFILLED

The fulfillment of this feast was in the book of Acts 1 and 2. Luke the beloved physician that followed Jesus ministry opened the book of Luke by addressing a gentleman by the name of Theophilus, whom we believe to be a Roman. He gave him instructions in the things that Jesus did.

*"Forasmuch as many have taken in hand to set forth in order a declaration of the things which are most surely believed among us, even as they delivered them unto us, which from the beginning were eyewitnesses, and ministers of the word;*

*It seemed good to me also, having perfect understanding of all things from the very first, to write unto thee in order, most excellent Theophilus, that thou mightest know the certainty of those things, wherein thou hast been instructed." (Luke 1:1-4)*

Here Luke spends twenty-four chapters instructing the most excellent Theophilus about the life of Jesus, from His birth to His ascension. All the activities of Jesus' ministry were discussed, and in the twenty-fourth chapter, he explained to him that Jesus had left and went into Heaven.

This looked like the conclusion of Jesus work on the earth, so Luke opens up the book of Acts by addressing the most excellent Theophilus again. This time he was reminding him that even though Jesus left us, His work would be continuing in the twelve men whom He had chosen as apostles in **Acts 1:1-8**.

*"The former treatise have I made, O Theophilus, of all that Jesus began to do and teach, until the day in which He was taken up, after that He through the Holy Ghost had given commandments unto the apostles whom He had chosen:*

*To whom also He shewed Himself alive after His passion by many infallible proofs, being seen of them forty days, and speaking of the things pertaining to the kingdom of God:*

*And, being assembled together with them, commanded them that they should not depart from Jerusalem, but wait for the promise of the Father, which, saith He, ye have heard of me.*

*For John truly baptized with water; but ye shall be baptized with the Holy Ghost not many days hence.*

*When they therefore were come together, they asked of Him, saying, Lord, wilt thou at this time restore again the kingdom to Israel?*

*And He said unto them, it is not for you to know the times or the seasons, which the Father hath put in His own power.*

*But ye shall receive power, after that the Holy Ghost is come upon you: and ye shall be witnesses unto me both in Jerusalem, and in all Judea, and in Samaria, and unto the uttermost part of the earth."*

Here Luke was telling the most excellent Theophilus that the acts of Jesus Christ were continuing as the Acts of the Apostles, through the twelve apostles that Jesus had chosen.

Jesus spent forty days on the earth after His resurrection, and told the apostle to tarry for a few more days and that they were going to experience the baptism of the Holy Ghost.

This experience happened to the apostle ten days after Jesus left. This made the fifty days and the day of Pentecost.

This corresponds with the exodus of the children of Israel from Egypt and their experience at Mount Sinai.

In the Old Testament, the blood of Christ was used symbolically as a covering for the children of Israel. They could not win a battle if the blood were not used.

After Adam and Eve sinned, they made coverings of leaves: Genesis 3:7.

*"And the eyes of them both were opened, and they knew that they were naked; and they sewed fig leaves together, and made themselves aprons." (Genesis 3:7)*

When God came down and saw this, He killed animals and made clothes of the skin and covered Adam and Eve's nakedness.

*Unto Adam also and to his wife did the Lord God make coats of skins, and clothed them." (Genesis 3:21)*

This was the first shadow of the crucifixion of Jesus Christ and it also shows that nothing that man does will ever be sufficient to cover himself. This also shows the innocent animals that didn't commit any sin, became the substitute for man. This became a pattern from Genesis to Malachi. Jesus Christ was also innocent and without sin, yet where man should have died, He took our place.

## THE BLOOD OF JESUS SECURED NOAH'S ARK

Some stories taught to us in Sunday school have left indelible impressions on us. One such story is the story of Noah and the Ark.

As we continue to grow in God and search His word, only then would we find deeper truths in His Word.

We know that every word that God speaks has a third dimension manifestation. Today, I now know that there is a first, second and third dimension in God. And that the level that we are on will determine our reception and understanding of God's word.

*"Deep calleth unto deep at the noise of thy waterspouts: all thy waves and thy billows are gone over me." (Psalms 42:7)*

This verse of scripture has a tremendous hidden revelation in it. It is telling us that while we pray and wait for an answer, God hears our prayer and has sent the answer. However, God could be transmitting on channel ten, while we are on channel two. We are just simply on the wrong frequency.

Having settled that the whole Bible is about Jesus, when we read whether it be the Old Testament or the New, we must ask the Holy Spirit to reveal to us what God is saying to us through Jesus Christ.

*And God said unto Noah, the end of all flesh is come before me; for the earth is filled with violence through them; and, behold, I will destroy them with the earth.*

*Make thee an ark of gopher wood; rooms shalt thou make in the ark, and shalt pitch it within and without with pitch." (Genesis 6:13-14)*

I grew up in High Rock, a small settlement in Grand Bahama, the Bahamas. A professional school teacher, I taught in some of the family islands in my country. I witnessed boat builders building new boats. As fishermen repair their boats after damages, I was told they were corking or pitching the boats so they would not sink.

I imagined Noah building the ark and was told to pitch it inside and out. He and his sons would go around this big boat making sure that every hole was closed with tar. We see there must have been some hard work in the preparation of this ship so that it will not sink. Today, I understand that the word 'pitch' in Hebrew is *Atonement*.

The day of Atonement was held every year for the people's sin. The Day of Atonement and its activities can be found in **Exodus 30:1-10.**

*"And thou shalt make an altar to burn incense upon: of shittim wood shalt thou make it.*

*A cubit shall be the length thereof, and a cubit the breath thereof; foursquare shall it be: and two cubits shall be the height thereof: the horns thereof shall be of the same.*

*And thou shalt overlay it with pure gold, the top thereof, and the sides thereof round about, and the horns thereof; and thou shalt make unto it a crown of gold round about.*

*And two golden rings shalt thou make to it under the crown of it, by the two corners thereof, upon the two sides of it shalt thou make it; and they shall be for places for the staves to bear it withal.*

*And thou shalt make the staves of shittim wood, and overlay them with gold.*

*And thou shall put it before the veil that is by the ark of the testimony, before the mercy seat that is over the testimony, where I will meet with thee.*

*And Aaron shall burn thereon sweet incense every morning: when he dresseth the lamps, he shall burn incense upon it.*

*And when Aaron lighteth the lamps at even, he shall burn incense upon it, a perpetual incense before the Lord throughout your generations.*

*Ye shall offer no strange incense thereof, nor burnt sacrifice, nor meat offering; neither shall ye pour drink offering thereon.*

*And Aaron shall make an Atonement upon the horns of it once in a year with the blood of the sin offering of Atonements: once in the year shall he make Atonement upon it throughout your generations: it is most holy unto the Lord."*

Now when we read how Noah pitched the ark, we see that the ark was covered outside and inside with the blood of Jesus. It was the blood of Jesus that kept the ark afloat symbolically.

# CHAPTER SIX

# THE BLOOD AND THE ANOINTING

Every believer that is called by God should be hungry for the anointing. There are different levels of the anointing and there are different types of anointing. Each type is on a different level. We have the Leprous Anointing, the Priestly Anointing, and the Kingly Anointing. The anointing is progressive, as one does not come without the other.

Leprosy in the Bible is symbolic of sin. The first anointing is the Leprosy Anointing, and it starts with the blood. No one can be saved without the blood of Jesus. We will revisit the story of the cleansing of the leppers to show the different types of anointing. The Leprous Anointing is found in **Leviticus, Chapter Fourteen.**

God gave Moses a procedure for the cleansing and anointing of the Leper.

*"And the Lord* spake *unto Moses, saying, this shall be the law of the leper in the day of his cleansing: he shall be brought unto the priest:*

*And the priest shall go forth out of the camp; and the priest shall look, and, behold, if the plague of leprosy be healed in the leper; then shall the priest command to take for him that is to be cleansed two birds alive and clean, and cedar wood, and scarlet, and hyssop:*

*And the priest shall command that one of the birds be killed in an earthen vessel over running water:*

*As for the living bird, he shall take it, and the cedar wood, and the scarlet, and the hyssop, and shall dip them and the living bird in the blood of the bird that was killed over the running water:*

*And he shall sprinkle upon him that is to be cleansed from the leprosy seven times, and shall pronounce him clean, and shall let the living bird loose into the open field."(Leviticus 14:1-7)*

This cleansing of the leper is symbolic of our Lord and Savior Jesus Christ leaving Heaven and coming to earth to redeem us from sin. The priest had to leave the camp because the leper was unclean and was not allowed to come into the camp.

Jesus had to leave Heaven because we were too sinful to come into Heaven.

The killing of the first bird is symbolic of the crucifixion of Jesus. As we look closely at this shadow or type, we will notice that it was the living bird that was dipped in the blood of the dead bird. These two birds represented one person, Jesus Christ. Even though He died, He is alive forevermore.

The sprinkling of the leper seven time points to the seven times and places during the crucifixion that Jesus shed His blood. After the leper was sprinkled, the priest would let the living bird fly away into the sky. We see clearly that this represented the resurrection of our Lord and Savior Jesus Christ.

Even though the leper was cleansed, he still had to stay outside the camp for seven days. These seven days represented rest. The leper now finds rest from his leprosy or freedom from sin. On the eighth day the cleansed leper would experience the anointing.

*"And on the eight day he shall take two he lambs without blemish, and one ewe lamb of the first year without blemish, and three tenth deals of fine flour for a meat offering, mingled with oil, and one log of oil.*

*And the priest that maketh him clean shall present the man that is to be made clean, and those things, before the Lord, at the door of the tabernacle of the congregation:*

*And the priest shall take one he lamb, and offer him for a trespass offering, and the log of oil, and wave them before for a wave offering before the Lord:*

*And he shall slay the lamb in the place where he shall kill the sin offering and the burnt offering, in the holy place: for as the sin offering is the priest's, so is the trespass offering: it is most holy:*

*And the priest shall take some of the blood of the trespass offering, and the priest shall put it upon the tip of the right ear of him that is to be cleansed, and upon the thumb of his right hand, and upon the right toe of his right foot:*

*And the priest shall take some of the oil, and pour it into the palm of his own left hand:*

*And the priest shall dip his right finger in the oil that is in his left hand, and shall sprinkle of the oil with his finger seven times before the Lord:*

*And of the rest of the oil that is in his hand shall the priest put upon the tip of the right ear of him that is to be cleansed, and upon the thumb of his right hand, and upon the great toe of his right foot, upon the blood of the trespass offering:*

*And the remnant of the oil that is in the priest's hand he shall pour upon the head of him that is to be cleansed: and the priest shall make an atonement for him before the Lord.*

*And the priest shall offer the sin offering, and make an atonement for him that is to be cleansed from his uncleanness; and afterward he shall kill the burnt offering:*

*And the priest shall offer the burnt offering and the meat offering upon the altar: and the priest shall make an atonement for him, and he shall be clean." (Leviticus 14:10-20)*

The cleansing of the leper and the anointing with oil is one of the most fascinating stories that point to the crucifixion of our Lord and Savior Jesus Christ.

Throughout this chapter, you will read about the sacrifice and the oil.

The Leprous Anointing is the very first anointing that a person receives. This happens at salvation. After the Leprous anointing is the Priestly anointing, and then the Kingly anointing. These stages are done in progression. You can not receive the priestly or the kingly anointing before receiving the leprous anointing.

## SAMUEL NEVER FORGOT THE BLOOD

The blood of Jesus is important for everything that was done unto God, and for God. If the blood was not seen, whatever was done was not received or sanctioned by God.

The first book of Samuel gives us one of the most accurate accounts of the blood and oil application. The beginning of First Samuel deals with the birth of Samuel and his presentation to the priest. Samuel's ministry began immediately after he was presented to Eli the priest. God gave Samuel as a spiritual son to Eli so that he would take over the priest office when Eli dies. Eli had two sons: Hophni and Phinehas, who were very wicked. They were rejected by God.

Samuel became a priest at a very early age and worked as a servant to the priest. Once a year his mother would take Samuel a cloak when she went to see him.

When Eli was ninety-eight years old, Israel was in a fierce battle against the Philistines. The Ark of the Covenant was stolen and Eli's two sons Hophni and Phinehas were killed.

While sitting in a chair, Eli was told that his sons were killed, so he just kept on rocking; but as soon as he heard that the Ark of the Covenant was stolen he fell from his chair backward, broke his neck, and died.

Samuel immediately became the official judge, priest and prophet of Israel. He judged Israel for forty years and every word he spoke came to pass. The Bible says that none of his words fell to the ground.

However, Samuel's sons did not follow in the steps of their father. They, like Eli's sons, did evil in the sight of God.

*"And it came to pass, when Samuel was old, that he made his sons judges over Israel.*

*Now the name of his firstborn was Joel; and the name of his second, Abiah: they were judges in Beerheba.*

*And his sons walked not in his ways, but turned aside after lucre, and took bribes, and perverted judgment.*

*Then all the elders of Israel gathered themselves together, and came to Samuel unto Ramah.*

*And said unto him, Behold, thou are old, and thy sons walk not in thy ways: now make us a king to judge us like all nations."(1Samuel 8:1-5)*

This saying displeased Samuel so he went unto the Lord in prayer. God answered Samuel and told him that the people did not reject him, but have rejected God.

*"And the Lord said unto Samuel, hearken unto the voice of the people in all that they say unto thee: for they have not rejected thee, but they have rejected me, that I should not reign over them.*

*According to all the works which they have done since the day that I brought them up out of Egypt even unto this day, wherewith they have forsaken me, and served other gods, so do they also unto thee.*

*Now therefore hearken unto their voice: howbeit yet protest solemnly unto them, and shew them the manner of the king that shall reign over them." (1 Samuel 8:7-9)*

Samuel protested and told the people everything that God had said. He told them how they, their children, and their possessions were going to belong to the king. He also told them that when they cry, because of the king that they have chosen, the Lord will not hear their prayer. The people refused to obey Samuel and decided that they will have a king.

I find this to be one of the most accurate accounts of God's creation of man with decision making ability.

God had already spoken to Jacob telling him that the King of Israel was coming through the tribe of Judah.

*"Judah, thou art he whom thy brethren shall praise: thy hand shall be in the neck of thy enemies; thy father's children shall bow down before thee.*

*Judah is a lion's whelp: from the prey, my son, thou art gone up: he stooped down, he couched as a lion, and as an old lion; who shall rouse him up?*

*The sceptre shall not depart from Judah, nor a law giver from between his feet, until Shiloh come; and unto Him shall the gathering of the people be." (Genesis: 49:8-10)*

This prophetic word coming out of Jacob's mouth just before he died clearly stated that a king was coming through the tribe of Judah, and that Jesus Christ (Shiloh) was also coming through the lineage of this king of Judah.

I am convinced that there are no mistakes in God. According to *Psalms 119:89,* God's word is forever settled in Heaven. God had settled in Himself that the first King of Israel was coming out of Judah.

In *Genesis 38,* Judah slept with his daughter-in-law, Tamar. We referred to the story of Judah and Tamar earlier, but before their story, God took an entire chapter in the book of Genesis and concentrated on Joseph.

In **Genesis 37,** God used the story of Jacob's love for his son Joseph, his brothers' jealousy, and their selling him into Egypt to preserve the entire nation of Israel.

This happened because in Deuteronomy 23:2 it is written,

*"A bastard shall not enter into the congregation of the Lord; even to his tenth generation shall he not enter into the congregation of the Lord."*

Let us not forget that we are still examining the blood of Jesus Christ and the anointing.

In the story of the children of Israel and their choosing Saul as king, they missed God's timing and the name of the tribe that God said the king of Israel was coming from.

Saul was from the tribe of Benjamin. Israel picked Saul because of his father's background, Saul's good behavior and stature. The Bible states that from Saul's shoulders and upwards he was higher than every one else in Israel.

God strongly objected to the children of Israel choosing a king. Since they missed His timing and tribal choice, He did not ask Samuel to go through the normal procedures of anointing someone for office. Samuel was in the high place where he built an altar to offer sacrifices to the Lord. It was on one of the feast of Israel, when

Samuel was offering sacrifices, that God orchestrated the meeting of Samuel and Saul.

Saul was led to Samuel after the loss of his father's asses. Saul did not know God's voice and perhaps would not have listened, even if he had known Jehovah and His ways of speaking. God had whispered in Samuel's ear that Saul was coming.

Samuel asked the cook to put aside the portion of the lamb shoulder, which was for the priest. This was being kept for Saul as a mark of respect.

You can read Saul's encounter with Samuel in **First Samuel,** Chapter **Nine.**

At the closing of the ninth chapter in the twenty-seventh verse, the prophet Samuel asked Saul to send his servant away so he could have some private time with him.

Saul did as Samuel requested and Samuel showed him the word of the Lord.

It is very important to note that Samuel offered sacrifice on one of Israel's feast days. God made it possible that Saul and Samuel meet.

Saul wanted to hear from God. He should have taken an animal sacrifice, which represented the blood of Jesus, but he took money that was not his own. No one hears from God without going through Jesus. No one offers God something that is not a sacrifice. It was always true that you did not go to see the man of God empty-handed. It was, and still is true that you can't access God without the blood of Jesus Christ.

Saul was picked by the natural eyes, and he was trying to receive from God through a natural way.

In the case of Samuel, God spoke to him in the high place while he was offering sacrifice. The Bible did not say which one of Israel feast Samuel was celebrating, but we do know that the sacrifice represents the blood of Jesus.

After Saul had sent his servants away, Samuel anointed Saul king over Israel.

*"Them Samuel took a vial of oil, and poured it upon his head, and kissed him, and said, is it not because the Lord had anointed thee to be captain over his inheritance?"(1Samuel 10-1)*

We all know the story of Saul and how he disobeyed God. Let us look at God's choice.

God had rejected Saul not because of the people's choice, but because of Saul's own choosing to do things his way.

After Saul had disobeyed God, Samuel decided that he wouldn't come any more to see Saul until the day of his death. After Saul's death Samuel continued to mourn for him, until the Lord spoke to him in chapter 16.

*"And the Lord said unto Samuel, how long wilt thou mourn for Saul, seeing I have rejected him from reigning over Israel? Fill thine horn with oil, and go, I will send thee to Jesse the Bethlehemite: for I have provided me a king among his sons." (1 Samuel 16:1)*

This made God's prophetic word accurate. We must remember the prophecy about Judah, Judah and Tamar's story, and the bastard not coming into the congregation until its tenth generation. **(Ruth 4:8-21)**

Jesse's name is mentioned as the ninth from Judah; beginning with Pharez, one of the twins that Judah had with his daughter-in-law.

Jesse's son David would be the tenth generation, and would become the first King of Judah.

*"And Samuel grew, and the Lord was with Him, and did let none of His words fall to the ground."(1Samuel 3:19)*

I have placed this verse of Scripture here to show you how God never changes His plans. Samuel was priest and judge over Israel for forty years. During those forty years, not once did he say something God told him and it did not come to pass. Yet, this true prophet of God told God that he could not go to Jesse's house and anoint one of his sons. He feared that Saul would have killed him.

This is the second time that fear is associated with Samuel. He became afraid when he had to deliver the truth about a vision concerning Eli's house, and now as a priest and judge of Israel.

I believe God permitted this fear to come on the man of God so that he could implement the blood of Jesus over Jesse's house; in particular, to have a blood covering for David before anointing Him with the oil.

*And Samuel said, how can I go? If Saul hears it, he will kill me. And the Lord said, take an heifer with thee, and say, I am come to sacrifice to the Lord.*

*And call Jesse to the sacrifice, and I will shew thee what thou shalt do: and thou shalt anoint unto me him whom I name unto thee.*

*And Samuel did that which the Lord spake, and came to Bethlehem. And the elders of the town trembled at his coming, and said, comest thou peaceably?*

*And he said, peaceably: I am come to sacrifice unto the Lord: sanctify yourselves, and come with me to the sacrifice. And he sanctified Jesse and his sons, and called them to the sacrifice." (1 Samuel 16:2-5)*

Here we see the prophet Samuel offering a sacrifice, which is a shadow of the crucifixion of Jesus Christ. After the blood comes the anointing. Praise God! If it comes any other way, it can not be real.

# CHAPTER SEVEN

# THE BLOOD COVERING

Today, we have thousands of religions, organizations, churches, apostles, prophets, pastors, teachers and evangelists. With this, we have various celebrations of feast days, conferences, revivals and seminars. There are various teachings of how to get rich, how to get power with God, and how to treat a friend, and many others. I believe that each person has a special call of God, yet God has not and will not receive anyone without the blood.

If you listen to various Christian television programs, there needs to be more emphasis on the blood of Jesus. All that we are or ever will be is hidden in Christ. **Colossians 3:3** says, *"For ye are dead, and your life is hid with Christ in God."*

The blood of Jesus seems to be too old fashioned for many of today's preachers: young and old. To me, I don't see where God ever changed the formula for accessing or receiving from Him.

We are going to examine the importance of using the blood of Jesus daily. Remember, after Adam and Eve sinned and they tried to cover themselves with leaves, the first thing that God did was He killed an innocent animal, made clothes of skin and covered their nakedness.

This showed us that man was never going to be able to do anything to pay for, or cover his own sins. It also points to the death of Jesus Christ. In **Genesis 3:15,** God promised that the Messiah will come one day as the seed of a woman.

Throughout the Bible, we see the blood of Christ applied symbolically whenever the nation of Israel went to war, or when an enemy was attacking them. It was even applied as a covering over family members.

We will take a look at just a few of these instances.

## THE BLOOD AS A PROTECTION FOR FAMILY MEMBERS

There are many stories that illustrate the importance of the blood covering for families. I will chose one of the oldest stories in the Bible; that is, the story of Job.

Job was the son of Issachar, and the grandson of Jacob.

*"And the sons of Issachar, Tola and Phuvah, and Job, and Shimron." (Genesis 46:13)*

Job was taught well by his ancestors: his father Issachar, his grandfather Jacob, and his great grandfather, Isaac. Whoever was Job's teacher, he learned very well and he applied what was taught.

The story of Job is a very popular one in the Bible. For those who have not read it, if they attend church they would have heard it preached, taught, or referred to.

Just to remind you, the Bible says that Job was the richest man in the East. As rich as he was, he never diverted from the principles taught to him by his ancestors.

*"And his sons went and feasted in their houses, every one his day; and sent and called for their three sisters to eat and to drink with them.*

*And it was so, when the days of their feasting were gone about, that Job sent and sanctified them, and rose up early in the morning, and offered burnt offerings according to the number of them all: for Job said, it may be that my sons have sinned, and cursed God in their hearts. Thus did Job continually." (Job 1:4-5)*

Back to the story of Job: we remember the dialog that satan had with God. When God asked satan where he came from he said, "From going to and fro the earth and from walking up and down in it."

God asked satan, *"Hast thou considered my servant Job, that there is none like him in the earth, a perfect and an upright man, one that feareth God, and escheweth evil?" (Job 1:8)*

satan's reply was that Job feared, love and obeyed God because God had a hedge around him, his house, and all that he had. satan also claimed that God had blessed the work of Job's hands, and He made sure that all of Job's substances were increased in the land.

God gave satan permission to touch Job's substances, but not to touch Job himself.

We read the story of Job so many times that we wonder what else new can be found. When we remind ourselves that the whole Bible is about Jesus, the Old and the New Testament, then everything takes on new meaning. Let's look a little closer.

*"And there was a day when his sons and his daughters were eating and drinking wine in their eldest brother's house:*

*And there came a messenger unto Job, and said, the oxen were plowing, and the asses feeding beside them:*

*And the Sabeans fell upon them, and took them away; yea, they have slain the servants with the edge of the sword; and I only am escaped alone to tell thee.*

*While he was yet speaking, there came also another, and said, the fire of God is fallen from Heaven, and hath burned up the sheep, and the servants, and consumed them; and I only am escaped alone to tell thee.*

*While he was yet speaking, there came also another, and said, the Chaldeans made out three bands, and fell upon the camels, and have carried them away, yea, and slain the servants with edge of the sword; and I only am escaped alone to tell thee." (Job 1:13-17)*

You may not have noticed that Job and his entire family were still alive, but he had no more animals.

satan had a strategy; he removed the animals first. This meant Job had no more animals to sacrifice. As long as there remained one animal, Job would sacrifice it to God, and he and his family and all that he had would have a blood covering.

Now we see what satan meant when he told God that He had a hedge around Job. It was the sacrifice what Job did every morning that put the hedge around him, his family, and his substances.

**In Job 1:19,** all of Job's children was killed. However, this could not have happened until all of the animals were killed, and the blood was removed.

When I think about this story and realized the power that the blood of Jesus has and that it took place when the blood was just a shadow or type, I get so excited because the law was not yet given when Job had his encounter.

satan could have killed all of Job's animals, for they were real animals, but when John the Baptist saw Jesus coming toward the Jordan River where he was baptizing he said, *"Behold the Lamb of God, which taketh away the sins of the world."*

John called Him the Lamb, and in Hebrews the apostle Paul called Him the last High Priest.

In the Old Testament, the priest had to take a lamb and sacrifice it to the Lord. Jesus Christ is both High Priest and Lamb.

As a lamb He died, but as the last High Priest He entered into the Holy of Holiest in the Tabernacle in Heaven. He entered with His own blood and sprinkled all the furniture in the Tabernacle in Heaven. This is why we can come boldly before the throne of God.

This excites me because satan removed the animals in the story of Job, but he cannot come near or touch the blood of our Lamb and High Priest, Jesus Christ. Hallelujah!

God spoke to Eliphaz and told him that He was against him and his two friends, because they had not spoken the right things about Him as Job did. He asked them to take animal sacrifices to Job and let Job pray for them, and only then will He accept them.

*"And it was so, that after the Lord had spoken these words unto Job, the Lord said to Eliphaz the Temanite, My wrath is kindled*

*against thee, and against thy two friends: for ye have not spoken of me the things that is right, as my servant Job hath.*

*Therefore take unto you now seven bullocks and seven rams, and go to my servant Job, and offer up for yourselves a burnt offering; and my servant Job shall pray for you: for him will I accept: lest I deal with you after your folly, in that ye have not spoken of me the things which is right, like my servant Job." (Job 42:7-8)*

Eliphaz and his two friends did as God commanded and took the animals to Job. As soon as Job offered the sacrifices to the Lord, the blood covering returned and God turned the captivity of Job around.

God restored his health and blessed him double. He doubled the amount of cattle, and he doubled the time Job lived. Job was seventy years when his trials started, and God gave him one hundred and forty more years. The days of Job were two hundred and ten years. He also had ten more children.

This all happened because someone knew how to apply the blood of Jesus.

## THE BLOOD PROTECTS FROM THE ENEMY

The Passover that was instituted in Egypt is one of the most powerful demonstrations of protection that one receives from the blood of Jesus. When the blood is applied in accordance with God and His word, God will always respond in a positive way.

As was said in a previous chapter, Samuel assumed the office of prophet, judge, and priest after Eli died. He judged Israel faithfully for forty years.

In the seventh chapter of the first book of Samuel, the children of Israel lost the Ark of the Lord to the Philistines. The Ark was made specifically for the nation of Israel, and it represented the presence of the Lord. Even though God killed thousands of the Philistines because they were not the legal owners of the Ark and had put idols in front of it; yet, because of Israel's backslidden condition He allowed the Ark to be in their possession for twenty years.

When the children of Israel cried unto the Lord, the prophet Samuel spake unto them and asked them to repent.

*"And Samuel spake unto all the house of Israel, saying, if ye do return unto the Lord with all your hearts, then put away the strange gods and Ashtaroth from among you, and prepare your hearts unto the Lord, and serve Him only: and He will deliverer you out of the hand of the Philistines." (1 Samuel 7:3)*

The children of Israel did as Samuel asked, and gathered themselves to Mizpeh. They fasted and poured themselves out before God, and confessed that they had sinned against the Lord.

The lords of the Philistines heard that the children of Israel were at Mizpeh, and they went up against them. This made the children of Israel afraid so they asked Samuel to pray to the Lord asking Him to save them out of the hand of the Philistines.

The next thing that happened shows the importance of the blood of Jesus.

*And Samuel took a suckling lamb, and offered it for a burnt offering wholly unto the Lord: and Samuel cried unto the Lord for Israel; and the Lord heard him.*

*And as Samuel was offering up the burnt offering, the Philistines drew near to battle against Israel: but the Lord thundered with a great thunder on that day upon the Philistines, and discomfited them; and they were smitten before Israel.*

*And the men of Israel went out of Mizpeh, and pursued the Philistines, and smote them, until they came under Bethcar.*

*Then Samuel took a stone, and set it between Mizpeh and Shen, and called the name of it Ebenezer, saying, hitherto hath the Lord helped us.*

*So the Philistines were subdued, and they came no more into the coast of Israel: and the hand of the Lord was against the Philistines all the days of Samuel." (1 Samuel 7:9-13)*

If you follow this story closely, you will see that the children of Israel fasted, prayed, and called upon Samuel asking him to pray to God for them.

Notice the first thing that Samuel did: he took a young lamb killed and offered it as a burnt offering to the Lord, and then he prayed. This shows clearly that there was no access to the Father with out the blood.

Samuel heard the people praying, but God heard Samuel's prayer. There had to be something the prophet knew that I believe still stands for today. We often say that God hears and answers prayer. I believe this; but that it will not happen without the blood of Jesus.

## VICTORY IN BATTLE BY THE BLOOD

In **Luke 11:2**, the disciples asked Jesus to teach them how to pray. Before Jesus gave them the pattern, He told them many things that they were not to do like the Pharisees. One is recorded in the Scripture text below.

*"But when ye pray, use not vain repetitions, as the heathen do: for they think that they shall be heard for their much speaking.*

*Be not ye therefore like unto them: for your Father knoweth what things ye have need of, before ye ask Him."(Matthew 6:7-8)*

In this passage of Scripture, I believe Jesus was telling us that the Father had a set-way as to how we must approach Him. He also knows what we need and what we ought to say before we receive them.

*"Likewise the Spirit also helpeth our infirmities: for we know not what we should pray for as we ought: but the Spirit itself maketh intercession for us with groanings which cannot be uttered.*

*And He that searcheth the hearts knoweth what is in the mind of the Spirit, because He maketh intercession for the saints according to the will of God." (Roman 8:26-27)*

There has to be a way for us to reach God. For the Holy Spirit is only going to make intercession for us in accordance with what He knows is the will of God.

Jesus said that the Father knows what you need before you ask Him.

*"Let us therefore come boldly unto the throne of Grace, that we may obtain mercy, and find Grace to help in time of need." (Hebrews 4:16)*

We are told that we can come boldly, but the priest had to go through many procedures before he could enter into the tabernacle that Moses built. After all the procedures, bells were tied to the skirt of the priest garment, and a rope was tied around him just in case he died. If the bells stopped ringing, it was a sign to the people that the priest did not meet God's standard and that he was dead. This put fear in everyone, especially the priest.

The apostle Paul continues to drive home the importance of the blood and what boldness it gives us.

*"Having therefore, brethren, boldness to enter into the holiest by the blood of Jesus, by a new and living way, which He hath consecrated for us, through the veil, that is to say, His flesh."(Hebrews 10:19-20)*

I have used all of these pointers to take you into the next powerful story concerning the blood of Jesus, and how it must be used when you are in a battle.

## NO BLOOD NO VICTORY

In **Judges 19,** there is a very interesting story about a certain Levite from Ephraim. He had taken a concubine from out of Bethlehem-Judah. His concubine played the harlot and ran away to her father's house in Bethlehem Judah. After staying for four months, her husband decided he would go after her and speak to her family about her returning home.

When the husband got to the father-in-law's house he was greeted warmly by his father-in-law, who asked him to stay; so he stayed three days. On the fourth day when he was about to leave he was again asked to spend another night. The second request was accepted, but when asked the third time, the man rejected it and left early the next day.

This Levite got as far as Jerusalem and was forced to spend the night with an old man who provided for them that night. During the night trouble came.

*"Now as they were making their hearts merry, behold, the men of the city, certain sons of belial,* (the devil) *beset the house round about, and beat at the door, and spake to the master of the house,*

*the old man, saying, bring forth the man that came into thine house, that we may know him.* (They were homosexuals)

*And the man, the master of the house, went out unto them, and said unto them, nay, my brethren, nay, I pray you, do not so wickedly; seeing that this man is come into mine house, do not this folly.*

*Behold, here is my daughter a maiden, and his concubine; them I will bring out now, and humble ye them, and do with them what seemeth good unto you: but unto this man do not so vile a thing.*

*But the men would not hearken to him: so the man took his concubine, and brought her forth unto them; and they knew her, and abused her all the night until the morning: and when the day began to spring, they let her go." (Judges 19:22-25)*

This story continues to develop, the concubine came at the dawning of the day and fell down at the door of the house where her husband was. She laid there until the breaking of the day. Her husbands rose up in the morning and opened the door of the house; and behold the woman, his concubine, was fallen down at the door of the house, and her hands were on the threshold.

The children of Israel then asked that the men who committed such wickedness be handed over so that they may be put to death, and the whole of Israel would be cleansed from this evil.

The children of Benjamin refused to comply with the request of Israel. The children of Benjamin decided that they were going to fight to protect those who committed such a crime.

This is where the hidden truth of the power in the blood of Jesus is revealed.

Before the children of Israel decided to do battle with the tribe of Benjamin, they enquired of the Lord.

*And the children of Israel arose, and went up to the house of God, and asked counsel of God, and said, which of us shall go up first to battle against the children of Benjamin? And the Lord said, Judah shall go up first.*

*And the children of Israel rose up in the morning, and encamped against Gibeah.*

*And the men of Israel went out to battle against Benjamin; and the men of Israel put themselves in array to fight against them at Gibeah.*

*And the children of Benjamin came forth out of Gibeah, and destroyed down to the ground of the Israelites that day twenty and two thousand men." (Judges 20:18-21)*

If you are like me, all kinds of questions must be going through you head. I looked at this Scripture and realized that the people prayed and God told them they could go and fight against Benjamin. God even told them who should go up first.

'Judah' means praise. Praise is a weapon, and must be used when going into a battle. When you are 'Praising', it is then that your hands are on the enemy's neck.

These people seemingly did what God told them to do, but were defeated by the enemy.

We must continue to read this developing story. The children of Israel encouraged themselves and sought the Lord a second time.

*"And the children of Israel went up and wept before the Lord until evening, and asked counsel of the Lord, saying, shall I go again to battle against the children of Benjamin my brother? And the Lord said, go up against him."*

*And the children of Israel came near against the children of Benjamin the second day.*

*And Benjamin went forth against them out of Gibeah the second day, and destroyed down to the ground of the children of Israel again eighteen thousand men; all these drew the sword.*

*"Then all the children of Israel, and all the people, went up, and came unto the house of the God, and wept, and sat there before the Lord, and fasted that day until even, and offered burnt offerings and peace offerings before the Lord.*

*And the children of Israel enquired of the Lord, (for the ark of the covenant of God was there in those days, and Phinehas, the son of Eleazar, the son of Aaron, stood before it in those days,) saying, shall I yet again go out to battle against the children of Benjamin my brother, or shall I cease? And the Lord said, go up; for to morrow I will deliver them into thine hand." (Judges 20:23-28)*

You should be more enlightened now. Israel had lost forty thousand men in two battles. They had prayed and gotten answers from God on two occasions. However, God never promised them victory until the third round.

Have you noticed that in the third battle they prayed, fasted, and offered up sacrifices? Please take note that God did not say what to do. The reason for this is because there are some things that God has already told us and are established as law with Him. God guaranteed them success only after He saw the blood.

*"And Israel set liers in wait round about Gibeah.*

*And the children of Israel went up against the children of Benjamin on the third day, and put themselves in array against Gibeah, as at other times.*

*And the children of Benjamin went out against the people, and were drawn away from the city; and they began to smite of the people, and kill, as at other times, in the highways, of which one goeth up to the house of God, and the other to Gibeah in the field, about thirty men of Israel.*

*And the children of Benjamin said, they are smitten down before us, as at the first. But the children of Israel said, let us flee, and draw them from the city into the highways.*

*And all the men of Israel rose up out of their place, and put themselves in array at Baaltamar: and the liers in wait of Israel came forth out of their places, even out of the meadows of Gibeah.*

*And there came against Gibeah ten thousand chosen men out of all Israel, and the battle was sore: but they knew not that evil was near them.*

*And the Lord smote Benjamin before Israel: and the children of Israel destroyed of the Benjamites that day twenty and five thousand and an hundred men: all these drew the sword."(Judges 20:29-35)*

When the blood of Jesus is applied, the strategy for victory is mapped out. Have you noticed that only ten thousand of Israel's men had to fight in this battle? The Bible says that the Lord smote the Benjamites.

This is what will happen when the blood of Jesus is applied.

# CHAPTER EIGHT

# THE BLOOD BRINGS FELLOWSHIP

The reason Jesus said 'My God, my God, why has thou forsaken Me was because it was the first time that Jesus was ever separated from the Father.

Throughout His life, Jesus tried to explain to the disciples how He and the Father were one, and that He was the expressed image of the Father.

In St. John's Gospel, Jesus told His disciples that there were many mansions in His Father's House. He told them that He was going to prepare a place for them and one day wherever He was they were going to come there too.

Jesus further said that where He was going they knew and the way they knew.

Thomas answered and said, **"Lord we know not whither thou goest; and how can we know the way?" (St. John 14:5)**

I love the way Jesus answered him. This settles the question of how one can get to God.

*"Jesus saith unto him, I am the Way, the Truth, and the Life: no man cometh unto the Father, but by me.*

*If ye had known me, ye should have known my Father also: and from henceforth ye know Him, and have seen Him."(St. John 14:6-7)*

Here Jesus points out the one way to the Father, and the oneness He had with the Father.

When Jesus said that He was the Way, the Truth, and the Life every Jewish leader and citizen understood this statement, but they did not accept it as it applies to Jesus.

They all knew about the Tabernacle Moses built in the wilderness. They knew it had three doors. The first door is the gate or entrance and is called the Way. The second door led to the Holy Place and is called the Truth. The third door, the veil is called the Life. Everything behind the veil is the life that we need.

Jesus was telling them that they needed three doors to meet with the Father, but He was those three doors in one.

Philip heard Jesus, but still saith unto Him, *"Lord show us the Father and it suffices us."(St. John 14:8)*

Jesus responded by saying in *"Have I been so long time with you, and yet hast thou not known me, Philip? he that hath seen me hath seen the Father; and how sayest thou then, shew us the Father?*

*Believest thou not that I am the Father, and the Father in me? the words that I speak unto you I speak not of Myself: but the Father that dwelleth in Me, He doeth the works.*

*Believe me that I am in the Father, and the Father in Me: or else believe Me for the very works sake." (St. John 14:9-11)*

Jesus has always called God His Father, which clearly shows His humanity. The angels do not know God as Father.

In the entire first chapter of Genesis we read, **"and God said."** In the second chapter of Genesis, God gave us a summary of His creation in the first three verses. After this we read, **"The Lord God."**

What is important about this is that in the first chapter, God was speaking to angels, who simply know Him as God. In the second chapter a relationship has been established with man, and we know Him as the Lord God.

You may ask what is so important about Jesus saying, **"My God, my God, why has thou forsaken me?"** Well, we need to know that it was the first time that Jesus was separated from His Father. He became sin for us and God revealed how Holy He was.

We believe that Jesus and the Father are one, and that God took on flesh and became man.

God is so holy that even when He became sin, He did not allow Himself in His presence, but He had to shed His blood so that man would be redeemed and have access to Him.

## GOD REMAINS THE SAME ABOUT THE BLOOD

Yes, we have beautiful schools, colleges, and programs. I listened to the President of the United States of America quoted Scriptures as they were signing the principles of peace. He said, "These are the children of Abraham, Isaac and Jacob. They must have peace." He was right. It is good he is quoting the Scripture; he needs to know the basics.

There are doctors and lawyers who read through the Bible. These lawyers must know the Bible as part of their course work, but they must also know the basics. There is absolutely no other way to God other than through His Son's blood.

All over the world people quote the Bible, but have they really gone through the blood of Jesus Christ? This is a reminder. When you are going through a crisis, remember that there is still power in the blood of Jesus Christ.

Abel brought a sacrifice. Cain also brought a sacrifice. Cain's sacrifice was for the priest and his family to eat. The priest's fruit is never brought as a sacrifice. The Bible says if you owned a farm, you could bring fruit to the priest, but you don't bring fruit to pay for your sins. The first sacrifice took place long before Cain.

When Adam and Eve were chased out of the garden, God killed an animal, and used its skin to cover their nakedness. That was the first sacrifice for sin. Adam and Eve made clothes of leaves, but it could not last.

What man does can not last. Our righteousness would not last.

Abel's sacrifice was accepted because he brought blood. Cain brought fruit to God, but God could not accept his sacrifice. God gave Cain another chance so he could bring in blood, but Cain did not offer God a blood sacrifice.

*"And in process of time it came to pass, that Cain brought of the fruit of the ground an offering unto the Lord.*

*And Abel, he also brought of the firstlings of his flock and of the fat thereof. And the Lord had respect unto Abel and to his offering: but unto Cain and to his offering He had not respect. And Cain was very wroth, and his countenance fell.*

*And the Lord said unto Cain, why art thou wroth? And why is thy countenance fallen?*

*If thou doest well, shalt thou not be accepted? And if thou doest not well, sin lieth at the door. And unto thee shall be his desire, and thou shall rule over him." (Genesis 4:3-7)*

How can we determine when God accepts an offering? They all took fire and lit the sacrifice according to the word. Elijah said, **"The God that answers by fire, let him be God."(1Kings 18:24).**

We have discovered that when sacrifices were made, God will come down on the sacrifice He accepts, and the fire would become bigger. The fire of God got into Abel's sacrifice because blood was shed, and it all pointed toward the sacrifice of Jesus Christ. God told Cain he should not be angry because He did not accept his sacrifice. He should have found out why his sacrifice was not accepted, and what God wanted.

According to our research, when God told Cain that sin lieth at the door, God had provided an animal sacrifice for Cain. Cain was given a second chance, but yet refused to give God what was already established in Heaven. There would be no forgiveness of sin without the blood. God is Boss, and will always be Boss.

When we pray to God for something and don't receive, we need to find out why we have not received it. God wants us to receive from Him. He wants to bless and deliver us.

The Bible says, *"Without faith it is impossible to please God, for he that cometh unto God must believe that He is and that He is the rewarder of them that diligently seek Him."*

When we come to God, we must believe God is what we are coming for. He is willing to give us what we are looking for. If we don't believe God has it, then it is no use going to Him. In order to have our prayers answered, we must remember these two things:-

1. We must go to God believing He has it.
2. We must go to God believing He wants to give it to us.

The Bible says if we doubt in our heart, we won't get our request answered. God told Cain to go outside and sacrifice the animal at the door. God had provided a sacrifice for Cain. He told him sin lieth at the door; meaning, a sacrifice for sin was out there. God gave Cain another chance, but Cain did not use it.

God gives us another chance to do the things He requires of us. He makes provisions for us; we must obey Him because He is the Boss.

# CHAPTER NINE

# THE BLOOD OF JESUS
# AND THE PROPHETS

*"But He was wounded for our transgressions, He was bruised for our iniquities: the chastisement of our peace was upon Him; and with His stripes we are healed." (Isaiah 53:5)*

Isaiah didn't say that he was wounded for your transgression. He included himself by saying **'our'** transgressions, bruised for **'our'** iniquities, the chastisement of **'our'** peace was upon Him, and with His stripes we are healed.

In **Isaiah 9:6** he didn't say, unto you a child is born; he said, **"For unto us a child is born, unto us a Son is given."**

Isaiah died over seven hundred years before Christ came the first time. Why did he include himself? Unless Christ had come, there was no hope for Abraham, Isaac, Jacob, Joseph, Ezekiel, Daniel, and the rest of the prophets.

**Hebrews Chapter 11,** is the hall of fame of Faith. This chapter deals with how by faith Abel, Enoch, Noah, Abraham, Sarah, and many others received from God.

Even though these people received from God by faith, yet Hebrews 11:13 states,

*"These all died in faith, not having received the promises, but having seen them afar off, and were persuaded of them,*

*and embraced them, and confessed that they were strangers and pilgrims on the earth.*"

So the question is: did the blood of Jesus wash away Isaiah, Abraham, Ezekiel, Daniel, Jeremiah, and the rest of the prophets' sins? I say yes. Isaiah said, He was wounded for our transgressions, and they all died in faith having not received the promise. What they did under the law was counted for righteousness.

They all waited in Abraham's Bosom until Jesus came to get them.

According to Bible history, Isaiah died by being sawn in half. He was placed in a log of wood; and with a hand saw was cut in half while yet alive. Isaiah died in faith expecting the promise.

There is still power in the blood of Jesus.

All of these prophets went into the under-world. There are only two that we know of who went to Heaven: Enoch and Elijah. The others were in the under world waiting in Abraham's bosom; waiting for the promise.

I believe one of the last prophets to step into Abraham's Bosom was John the Baptist. Also, I believe that he told them how he saw the Lamb. How he baptized Him in the River Jordan, and how he saw the Spirit descending upon Him like a dove.

John continues to relate his story by telling them he knew that it was Jesus, for whom he was sent to prepare the way. He knew this because God, who sent him to baptize, told him that He was going to give him a sign as to how to recognize the Messiah.

The one that he sees the Spirit descending upon, and remaining on, is the one that will have the Spirit of God without measure.

Isaiah could have written, He was wounded for 'his' transgressions because of what the apostle John wrote concerning the people who will worship the Antichrist. Isaiah could have written this because the lamb was slain before the foundation of the world. **Revelation 13:8** says,

*"And all that dwell upon the earth shall worship him, whose names are not written in the book of life of the Lamb slain from the foundation of the world."*

There was a ceremony, a dedication service. God dedicated the earth to Jesus. The Bible says the stone which the builders rejected became the head of the corner. That was the dedication service for His earth.

I believe this is one of the reasons why God is going to allow Jesus Christ to reign on this earth for 1,000 years upon the throne of David in Jerusalem, and then reign forever.

God allowed seven people in the Old Testament to live over 900 years. Methuselah, the eldest, lived 969 years. The other six were: Adam, Seth, Enos, Cainan, Jared, and Noah. Adam lived 930 years. Seth walked on the earth for 912 years. Enos lived for 905 years. Cainan lived for 910 years. Jared lived for 962 years, and Noah lived for 950 years.

Jesus will still be the only one to walk and reign on the earth for the longest period of time; one thousand years, and forever.

*"Then the Lord answered Job out of the whirlwind, and said, who is this that darkeneth counsel by words without knowledge?*

*Gird up now thy loins like a man: for I will demand of thee, and answer thou me.*

*Where wast thou when I laid the foundations of the earth? Declare, if thou hast understanding.*

*Who hath laid the measures thereof, if thou knowest? Or who hath stretched the line upon it?*

*Whereupon are the foundations thereof fastened? Or who laid the corner stone thereof;*

*When the morning stars sang together, and all the sons of God shouted for joy?" (Job 38: 1- 7)*

When the earth was made there was a corner stone laid. Even though Jesus Christ was rejected, He is still the head of the corner.

*"The stone which the builders refused is become the head stone of the corner.*

*This is the Lord's doing; it is marvelous in our eyes."(Psalms 118:22-23)*

The prophet Zechariah confirmed to us that when Israel would have gone through all of its trials, and is faced with persecution from the antichrist and other nations of the world, Jesus will be the one that will come and rescue them.

*"And I will pour upon the house of David, and upon the inhab-
itants of Jerusalem, the Spirit of Grace and of Supplications: and
they shall look upon Me whom they have pierced, and they shall
mourn for him, as one mourneth for his only son, and shall be in
bitterness for him, as one that is in bitterness for his firstborn."
(Zechariah 12:10)*

Up until Jesus Christ, it is amazing how for the sixty-six books
of the Bible people always rejected the one God sends. Even though
rejected, the people deliverance was in the person that God sent.

God does not live in time, yet in the book of Genesis he used one
week to restore the earth.

Since we have established the fact that God's word is forever
settled in Heaven, and that He has finished everything at the
beginning, then the question comes: Why did He use time in the
creation?

I believe the reason that God used time was because He was
going to establish His eternal purpose in man in time.

God took one week and gave man one week. In the one week,
the seventh day belongs to God.

Each day in man's week was going to be as a thousand years.
From Adam to Noah, one thousand years or one day had passed.
From Noah to Abraham, one thousand years or the second day
passed. From Abraham to King David, another thousand years
passed. This was the third day in man's week. From King David to
Jesus Christ, another thousand years passed, and we came into the
fourth day of man's week.

After Jesus' death on the cross the fifth, sixth, and seventh day of
man's week remained. We know that the fifth and the sixth day are
gone and we are now in the seventh day.

However, we want to concern ourselves with the Lamb slain
before the foundation of the world.

We see that Jesus showed up on the fourth day of man's week
and was crucified in that day, yet the Bible says that He is the Lamb
slain before the foundation of the world. Here God is showing that
He knows everything about us, and even the things that He has
finished concerning us will be manifested in time.

Now we can clearly see why Isaiah says that He was wounded for our transgressions.

We can see why the prophets all died in faith having not received the promise. Praise God, the promise came and took them out of Abraham's bosom. They became a part of the first fruit that Jesus took with Him to Heaven and presented to the Father when He was resurrected from the dead.

# CHAPTER TEN

# ALL CHILDREN HAVE THEIR FATHER'S BLOOD

*"For the life of the flesh is in the blood: and I have given it to you upon the altar to make an atonement for your souls: for it is the blood that maketh an atonement for the soul."*
*(Leviticus 17:11)*

The blood was so important to God that He made it mandatory that if anyone drinks blood or eats flesh with blood shall be cut off.

*"Therefore I said unto the children of Israel, no soul of you shall eat blood, neither shall any stranger that sojourneth among you eat blood.*

*And whatsoever man there be of the children of Israel, or of the strangers that sojourn among you, which hunteth and catcheth any beast or fowl that may be eaten; he shall even pour out the blood thereof, and cover it with dust.*

*For it is the life of all flesh; the blood of it is for the life thereof: therefore I said unto the children of Israel, Ye shall eat the blood of no manner of flesh: for the life of all flesh is the blood thereof: whosoever eateth it shall be cut off."(Levitcus17:12-14)*

This command carries such a prophetic word. Eternal life for all mankind is in the blood of Jesus Christ.

It's amazing that no matter how a daughter may look like her mother, or grand mother or even an aunt, if she is taken to the doctor and a paternity test is done, she would have her father's blood. Sons and daughters would have the blood of their father.

I believe in Jesus Christ's blood because Adam came from the dust and returned to the dust. However, I also believe that since Adam had no earthly father, his blood came directly from the Heavenly Father.

Adam's blood was pure and clean, but sin contaminated it.

Like Adam, Jesus also has his Father's blood. However, unlike Adam, He never sinned. God sent Him in a womb that was never touched by man. He rode on a donkey that was never ridden, and he was laid in a tomb that was never used.

In addition to these facts, Jesus did not do anything unless He saw his Father doing it first.

Mary Magdalene came to embalm Jesus Christ because she thought his body would rot. The Psalmist David said in Psalms 16:10,

*"For thou wilt not leave my soul in hell; neither wilt thou suffer thine Holy One to see corruption." (Psalms 16:10)*

David died, was buried, and saw corruption; so he was not speaking about himself. The angel Gabriel told Mary that the thing that was going to happen to her was of the Holy Ghost.

Joseph was Jesus' stepfather. I believe that Jesus is the only virgin birth and this makes Him the fulfillment of the prophecy in **Genesis 3:15**, which said that the seed of the woman shall come and bruise the head of the serpent, which is the devil himself.

If Jesus was still in the grave, His body would still be fresh to this day because the Bible says in **St. John 1:14**, *"And the Word was made became flesh, and dwelt among us, and we beheld His glory, the glory as of the only begotten of the Father, full of Grace and Truth."(St. John 1:14)*

The Word will never pass away.

Earlier, we visited the story of Jesus going to prepare a place for us. We settled that lucifer had taken his rebellion into Heaven and messed up the place we have to go through to access the Father.

Jesus went to fix this place, which is really the Temple of God in Heaven, according to **Hebrews 9:11-12.**

*"But Christ being come an High Priest of good things to come, by a greater and more perfect tabernacle, not made with hands, that is to say, not of this building;*
*Neither by the blood of goats and calves, but by His own blood had He entered in once into the Holy Place, having obtained eternal redemption for us."*

While John was on the Isles of Patmos, he was given a revelation of Jesus Christ. This was after He was resurrected from the dead. According to Revelation, Chapter One, he saw Jesus in the Tabernacle in Heaven.

*"And I turned to see the voice that spake with me. And being turned, I saw seven golden candlesticks;*
*And in the midst of the seven candlesticks one like unto the Son of man, clothed with a garment down to the foot, and girt about the paps with a golden girdle.*
*His head and His hair were white like wool, as white as snow; and His eyes were as a flame of fire;*
*And His feet like unto fine brass, as if they burned in a furnace; and His voice as the sound of many waters.*
*And He had in His right hand seven stars: and out of His mouth went a sharp two edged sword: and His countenance was as the sun shineth in his strength.*
*And when I saw Him, I fell at His feet as dead. And He laid His right hand upon me, saying unto me, Fear not; I am the First and the Last:*
*I am He that liveth, and was dead; and behold, I am alive for evermore, Amen: and have the keys of Hell and of Death.*
*Write the things which thou hast seen, and the things which are, and the things which shall* **be hereafter.***"(Revelation 1:12-19)*
The apostle Paul describes how God looked around Heaven and decided He needed some blood to cleanse Heaven. He saw that there was no one in Heaven with blood. He had already concluded that

without the shedding of blood there would be no remission for sin. This is one of the reasons why He decided to wrap Himself in flesh and come down and be born of a virgin.

This is what makes the blood of Jesus so very powerful. If all children have their father's blood, then the blood that was flowing through Jesus' vein was the very blood of God His Father.

## THE SEARCH FOR THE SEED OF THE WOMAN

For 4,000 years, the devil was destroying families looking for the seed of a woman. He messed up Cain. God gave Adam another son named Seth. Noah came on the scene and the devil thought that God would use the younger son, so he got Ham to laugh at his father's nakedness.

The devil thought maybe God would use Abraham oldest son Ishmael, but God used the youngest son Isaac; the covenant child and only son born to Abraham and Sarah.

Isaac had twin boys, so the devil said maybe God will go back to the older son because he just used the younger one. The devil was frustrated because he did not understand that God was going to use the seed of the woman. He did not understand the Scripture when God spoke to Abraham about Jesus coming through his descendants. God used the words sand and stars, combined them, and still said his Seed.

This caught my attention because God could have said *seeds*, but He knew that the future of Abraham's race was wrapped up in one Seed, the Seed of a woman.

*"That in blessing I will bless thee, and in multiplying I will multiply thy seed as the stars of Heaven, and as the sand which is upon the sea shone; and thy Seed shall possess the gate of his enemies;*

*And in thy Seed shall all the nations of the earth be blessed; because thou hast obeyed my voice." (Genesis 22:17-18)*

The devil was confused because he didn't understand that Jesus was going to be the Seed of Abraham, the Seed of Isaac, the Seed Jacob, the Seed of David, the Seed of a woman, and still not the Seed of a man.

Jacob had twelve sons; this really confused the devil. God did not use Reuben the eldest or Benjamin the youngest. Instead, He used Joseph. All this time, the devil was looking for the Seed who was going to bruise his head.

This continued all the way to the book of Matthew. The angels of the Lord came down and announced to the shepherds: unto us is born this day in the city of David a Saviour who is Christ the Lord.

Immediately, after satan heard this he set out to have Jesus killed. He thought he had succeeded when Jesus died on the cross.

As was stated in Chapter One of First Corinthians, the mystery of the cross was hidden from principalities. The devil did not expect Jesus Christ, his Boss from heaven, to be the one that he had to face; after all Jesus created him as a holy angel.

*"Howbeit we speak wisdom among them that are perfect: yet not the wisdom of this world, nor of the princes of this world, that come to nought:*

*But we speak the wisdom of God in a mystery, even the hidden wisdom, which God ordained before the world unto our glory:*

*Which none of the princes of this world knew: for had they known it, they would not have crucified the Lord of glory."(1 Corinthians 2: 6-8)*

It is wonderful that God put something in place, made it law, and let it become settled with Him. One of the laws is that all children will have their father's blood. This makes the blood of Jesus the blood of His Father, and it has the power to wash away our sin.

# CHAPTER ELEVEN

# THE BLOOD DOES
# A COMPLETE WORK

J esus Christ did a complete work when he shed his blood. It was so complete that it actually did something for heaven.

*"And I turned to see the voice that spake with me. And being turned, I saw seven golden candlesticks;*

*And in the midst of the seven candlesticks one like unto the son of man, clothed with a garment down to the foot, and girt about the paps with a golden girdle.*

*His head and His hairs were white like wool, as white as snow; and His eyes as a flame of fire;*

*And His feet like unto fine brass, as if they burned in a furnace; and His voice as the sound of many waters.*

*And He had in His Right Hand seven stars: and out of His mouth went a sharp two edged sword: and His countenance was as the sun shineth in his strength." (Revelation 1:12-16)*

This passage of Scripture is taken from the book of Revelation. The revelation of Jesus Christ was given to the apostle John while he was on the Isle of Patmos.

John was hearing the voice and was describing the person from whom the voice came. He said He was in the midst of the golden candlesticks. Candlesticks are found in the second dimension of the

Tabernacle. Jesus had already been resurrected from the dead, and was now in the Tabernacle in Heaven.

This became very clear to John for he was able to match the Tabernacle with the one that Moses built in the Old Testament. The original Tabernacle is in Heaven, and the Tabernacle that Moses built was patterned after it.

Jesus Christ's blood not only washed away our sins, it actually cleansed Heaven. When Jesus Christ was on the cross, satan and the people wanted Him to shed blood. Even God was saying, bleed Son; I need your blood to cleanse heaven.

This is a reason why Isaiah said that it pleased the Lord to bruise Him.

*"Yet it pleased the Lord to bruise Him; He hath put Him to grief: when thou shalt make His soul an offering for sin, He shall see His seed, He shall prolong His days, and the pleasure of the Lord shall prosper in His hand." (Isaiah 53:10)*

The apostle John on the Isle of Patmos saw Jesus in the Tabernacle in Heaven.

The apostle Paul, in the books of Hebrews through Revelation, saw what Jesus did with His blood in Heaven in the Tabernacle. When John was on the Isle of Patmos for preaching the gospel, God showed him Heaven and the condition of the churches on the earth.

**Revelation Chapters 1, 2, and 3** deals with the church. In the fourth chapter, the church is raptured.

In the Tabernacle that Moses built there were an outer court, a brazen altar of sacrifice, and a laver. In the inner court, or the Holy Place were the seven candlesticks called the Menorah, the table of shew bread, and the golden altar of incense.

A veil separated the Holy Place from the Holy of Holies. Behind the veil in the Holy of Holies was the Ark of the Covenant.

*"Thou art the anointed cherub that covereth: and I have set thee so: thou wast upon the holy mountain of God; thou hast walked up and down in the midst of the stones of fire." (Ezekiel 28:14)*

**Isaiah 14:13** also gave an account of lucifer in the holy mountain of God.

*"For thou hast said in thine heart, I will ascend into Heaven, I will exalt my throne above the stars of God: I will sit also upon the mount of the congregation, in the sides of the north." (Isaiah 14:13)*

This is where the whole of Heaven goes to worship God. lucifer was praise leader in Heaven and along with the congregation had to pass through the temple of God to get to the Holy Mountain of God for worship. It was this temple that got messed up; lucifer thought he was the high priest of Heaven because he had for his covering most of the precious stones that was on the High Priest's robe. We will revisit this story again.

The Kingdom of God Jesus established on the earth is a pattern of the Kingdom of Heaven where the Father lives and rules forever.

*"In the year that king Uzziah died I saw also the Lord sitting upon a throne, high and lifted up, and His train filled the temple.*

*Above it stood the seraphims: each one had six wings; with twain he covered his face, and with twain he covered his feet and with twain he did fly.*

*And one cried unto another, and said, Holy, Holy, Holy, is the Lord of Hosts: the whole earth is full of His glory.*

*And the posts of the door moved at the voice of him that cried, and the house was filled with smoke." (Isaiah 6:1-4)*

In Heaven, God has books. Our names and the activities of our members are recorded in these books.

*"My substance was not hid from thee, when I was made in secret, and curiously wrought in the lowest part of the earth.*

*Thine eyes did see my substance, yet being unperfect; and in thy book all my members were written, which in continuance were fashioned, when as yet there was none of them." (Psalms 139:15-16)*

We have to give an account for the things we do with our members and the things we say with our mouth. According to **Ecclesiastes 5-6,** *"Suffer not thy mouth to cause thy flesh to sin; neither say thou before the angel, that it was an error: wherefore should God be angry at thy voice, and destroy the work of thine hands?"*

*"Let not your heart be troubled: ye believe in God, believe also in me.*
*In my Father's House are many mansions: if it were not so, I would have told you. I go to prepare a place for you.*
*And if I go and prepare a place for you, I will come again, and receive you unto myself; that where I am, there ye may be also.*
*And whither I go ye know, and the way ye know." (St. Johns 14:1-4)*

For many years this passage of Scripture has been misinterpreted. Jesus promised to prepare us a place. He didn't go to prepare a mansion. In God's house there are many mansions. They were there before the foundation of the world. He went to prepare us a place, so we can have access to the Father.

John saw a temple in Heaven with all the furniture he was familiar with, and matched them with the ones that were in the tabernacle that Moses built.

The temple in heaven is the place where lucifer would pass through to lead the congregation of Heaven to the holy mountain of God for worship. This is where lucifer took his rebellion and messed up the place. lucifer's desire has not changed; his desire for worship got him kicked from Heaven. He tried to get into the Holy mountain of God, where God sits on His throne and where He is worshipped.

*"For thou hast said in thine heart, I will ascend into Heaven, I will exalt my throne above the stars of God: I will sit also upon the mount of the congregation, in the sides of the north." (Isaiah 14:13)*

Before Christ comes, lucifer will embody the antichrist and once again go to Jerusalem, get into the temple and defiled it.

This place that lucifer messed up, is the place that Jesus went to prepare so that we can have access to the Father. This is why the blood of Jesus didn't just wash away our sins it also cleansed Heaven.

God, who cannot go back on His word, declared that there would be no remission for sin without the shedding of blood. He looked around in Heaven and there was no one with blood.

Since all children have their father's blood, then the blood that was in Jesus' vein was the blood of His Father.

*"Neither by the blood of goats and calves, but by His own blood He entered in once into the Holy place, having obtained eternal redemption for us." (Hebrews 9:12)*

Jesus took His own blood into Heaven, sprinkled all of the furniture, and fixed the place.

I believe that this is one of the most powerful features about the blood of Jesus. Also, I believe that this was the main reason the saints from Abel to Christ stayed in Abraham's Bosom. They had no access to the Father without the blood of Jesus. Even though they all died in faith, they had to wait until Jesus' blood was shed and the place fixed before they could meet with the Father.

*"Wherefore He saith, when He ascended up on high, He led captivity captive, and gave gifts unto men." (Ephesians 4:8)*

These captives were held by satan in Paradise, under the earth, until Christ conquered Death, Hell, and the Grave.

*"For as much then as the children are partakers of flesh and blood, He also himself likewise took part of the same; that through death He might destroy him that had the power of death, that is, the devil;*

*And deliver them who through fear of death were all their lifetime subject to bondage.*

*For verily He took not on Him the nature of angels; but He took on Him the seed of Abraham." (Hebrews 2:14-16)*

God cannot lie, and He always honors His word. He had already stated that man was going to have dominion over His work on the earth.

*And God said, let us make man in our image, after our likeness: and let them have dominion over the fish of the sea, and over the fowl of the air, and over the cattle, and over the earth, and over every creeping thing that creepeth upon the earth." (Genesis 1:26)*

God confirms this in **Psalms 8:4-6,**
*"What is man, that thou art mindful of him? And the son of man, that thou visitest him?*
*For thou has made him a little lower than the angels, and hast crowned him with glory and honour.*
*Thou madest him to have dominion over the works of thy hands; thou hast put all things under his feet."*

The word of God stated that Jesus did not take on the nature of angels but the seed of Abraham. This was letting us know that when Adam fell he lost dominion to the devil, but God had already said that dominion was going to be taken by man. This is the reason that God came as a man and not as an angel.

There is nowhere in God's word that He said angels were going to take dominion instead, He said man will. Jesus Christ became the perfect man and defeated the devil, through perfection, in the same office the devil had stolen. If God had come into the world any other way and taken dominion, He would have been illegal and would have gone against His own word.

This shows the wisdom of God and the unchanging ways that kept Him committed to His word. If God had sent Him as a spirit or an angel, this would have been the first spirit or spirit being He would have made with blood. Instead, God decided to abide by His own word. He said I will become man and I will have my own blood and I will be able take dominion; only this time, My word is going to be made flesh and dwell among men.

Adam came from the dust and had to return to the dust to fulfill the law. The Second Adam did not come from the dust, and the dust could not hold what was not its own.

When Mary Magdalene and the other women came to the sepulcher to embalm Jesus, they did not know what I know today. If Jesus did not get up from the grave, He would have still been there today. He could not see corruption.

Jesus tells a story of two beggars: one was poor and begged in this life; the other was rich and begged in eternity. Jesus gave an account of both beggars' lives on earth and in eternity. He also gave their location in the underworld after their deaths.

*"And in hell he lift up his eyes, being in torments, and seeth Abraham afar off, and Lazarus in his bosom.*

*And he cried and said, Father Abraham, have mercy on me, and send Lazarus, that he may dip the tip of his finger in water and cool my tongue; for I am tormented in this flame." (Luke 16:23-24)*

Lazarus had joined the captives and was also led out by Jesus. Jesus went into the underworld and brought out all those who died in faith, who not having received the promise waited for it in Abraham's Bosom.

While Jesus was three days in the grave, He knew exactly where He was going. The Scribes and the Pharisees asked Him to show them a sign. His answer to them is found in **Matthew 12:39-40.**

*"But He answered and said unto them, an evil and adulterous generation seeketh after a sign; and there shall no sign be given to it, but the sign of the prophet Jonas:*

*For as Jonas was three days and three nights in the whale's belly; so shall the Son of man be three days and three night in the heart of the earth."*

Jesus told them that He was going to spend three days and three nights in the underworld. He used this time to lead captivity captive. They were still alive in soul and spirit since their physical death, but were held captive. This proves the immortality of the soul. Jesus could have let the captive become extinct souls, but instead their souls were very much alive.

When a Christian dies, he or she does not go into the lower parts of the earth to be held captive, but goes to Heaven to live and await the resurrection of the body.

*"We are confident, I say, and willing rather to be absent from the body, and to be present with the Lord."(2 Corinthians 5:8)*

The apostle Paul questioned the profitability of his staying on earth in comparison with living in Heaven. His conclusion was that he had everything to benefit if he went to Heaven, but God would profit if he stayed on earth.

*"For me to live is Christ, and to die is gain.*
*But if I live in the flesh, this is the fruit of my labour: yet what I shall choose I wot not.*
*For I am in a strait betwixt two, having a desire to depart, and to be with Christ; which is far better: Nevertheless to abide in the flesh is more needful for you." (Philippians 1:21-24)*

Here the apostle Paul put God and people first. He could have chosen to stay on earth and continue to work for the Lord, or go to Him in Heaven.

This was only made possible through the blood of Jesus. When He went down into Paradise, He left it clean and closed it up completely.

Now the apostle Paul can talk about going directly to Heaven whenever he leaves this earth.

*"But ye are come unto mount Sion, and unto the city of the living God, the Heavenly Jerusalem, and to an innumerable company of angels,*
*To the general assembly and church of the firstborn, which are written in Heaven, and to God the judge of all, and to the spirits of Just men made perfect." (Hebrews 12:22-23)*

A reference is made below to the children of Israel and the touching of the mount in the wilderness. This took place with the sound of a trumpet and the voice of words that those who heard it entreated that no further word be spoken to them.

*"For ye are not come unto the mount that might be touched, and that burned with fire, nor unto blackness, and darkness, and tempest,*
*And the sound of a trumpet, and the voice of words; which voice they that heard intreated that the word should not be spoken to them any more:*
*For they could not endure that which was commanded, and if so much as a beast touch the mountain, it shall be stoned, or thrust through with a dart:*
*And so terrible was the sight, that Moses said, I exceedingly fear and quake." (Hebrews 12:18-21)*

It is made very clear that there is a vast difference of the activities at Mount Sinai and Mount Zion, or Heaven. It is said that the spirits of just men were made perfect. This was done by the shed blood of Jesus.

*"And to Jesus the mediator of the new covenant, and to the blood of sprinkling, that speaketh better things than that of Abel." (Hebrews 12:24)*

The first record of blood offered was Abel. His offering was accepted by God. This is the reason that his name is used. Every one who offered similar blood sacrifices were received by God. This points to the crucifixion of Jesus Christ.

However, the blood that was offered by Abel and others of the old covenant could not make man's spirit perfect. Also, it could not get man into the Heavenly Mount Zion.

According to Hebrews Chapters Nine and Twelve, Jesus took His blood and sprinkled the furniture in the Tabernacle in the Heavenly Mount Zion. This gave man access to the Father.

The apostle Peter said that he was sprinkled with this same blood, and became sanctified.

*"Peter an apostle of Jesus Christ, to the strangers scattered through out Pontus, Galatia, Cappadocia, Asia, and Bithynia, Elect according to the foreknowledge of God the Father, through sanctification of the Spirit, unto obedience and sprinkling of the blood of Jesus Christ: Grace unto you, and peace, be multiplied."* *(1Peter 1:1-2)*

I believe, this is the place where Jesus sprinkled His blood in the Tabernacle in Heaven that the works of the saints are being tried. If we do things in the flesh, our work will burn.

# CHAPTER TWELVE

# WHAT IS DONE
# FOR CHRIST WILL LAST

The blood of Jesus Christ prepared the place in Heaven that lucifer had messed up. I believe that when we get to Heaven, this is the place where our works will be tried. I also believe that it is being tried now.

Long before man was created lucifer was looking for worship. This is the reason he was kicked out of Heaven. In **Isaiah 14:13,** he said that he was going to exalt his throne above the stars of God, and that he was going to sit upon the mount of the congregation, in the sides of the north.

From our study of God's word, we know that Heaven is in the North, and when we worship God our praise and worship goes North.

*"Unto Thee, O God, do we give thanks, unto Thee do we give thanks: for that thy name is near thy wondrous works declare.*

*When I shall receive the congregation I will judge uprightly.*

*The earth and all the inhabitants thereof are dissolved: I bear up the pillars of it.*

*I said unto the fools, deal not foolishly: and to the wicked, lift not up the horn:*

*Lift not up your horn on high: speak not with a stiff neck.*

*For promotion cometh neither from the east, nor from the west, nor from the south.*

*But God is the Judge: He putteth down one, and setteth up another.*

*For in the hand of the Lord there is a cup, and the wine is red; it is full of mixture; and He poureth out of the same: but the dregs thereof, all the wicked of the earth shall wring them out, and drink them.*

*But I will declare for ever; I will sing praises to the God of Jacob.*

*All the horns of the wicked also will I cut off: but the horns of the righteous shall be exalted." (Psalms 75:1-10)*

God talks about receiving the congregation and how He will judge them. He is talking about how foolish it is for people to do anything in the flesh. God judges everything that we do.

God pointed out that promotions come from Him in the North or from the location in Heaven, depending on whether the individual is doing something in the flesh or in the Spirit.

We have heard both God and lucifer talked about the North, thus we have concluded that Heaven is in the North.

God has made it plain in Psalms that He also pays attention to persons who are proud and stiff necked in their presentation to Him.

From the first man Adam in the Garden of Eden to the church in Revelation, God has demonstrated that nothing can be accomplished in the flesh. In the forty ninth chapter of Genesis God hid this in the prophecy of Jacob to his children.

I have completed a sermon series titled "The Twelve Things The Church Must Go Through." With the exception of Simeon and Levi, these sermons deal with Jacob sons individually.

In Genesis Chapters 34 and 49, whenever Jacob spoke to or about his children he would list each child separately, except for Simeon and Levi who were listed together. This is because Simeon and Levi represent the flesh and the spirit. No one can leave their flesh and spirit home; wherever one go the other goes with it. The flesh and the spirit never agreed with each other, and only the spirit can get saved.

Whenever a church door is opened and the people begin to praise and worship God, you are either producing a Simeon [Flesh] or Levi [Spirit] praise. Now you understand why both God and lucifer are paying attention to the congregation in the North [Heaven].

Let us now look at Genesis Chapter 49. In the third and fourth verses, Reuben is mentioned by himself. In the eighth through the twelfth verse, we read about Judah; the thirteenth verse is about Zebulun, the fourteenth and fifteenth verses Issachar is referred to. The sixteenth through eighteenth, Dan's future is spelled out. Verse nineteen, refers to Gad; verse twenty to Asher, and verse twenty-one to Naphtali. Joseph's future is foretold in verses twenty-two through twenty-six; and verse twenty-seven singles out Benjamin.

If you notice, I did not mention Simeon and Levi. This was intentional so that you can examine verses five through seven of this chapter and see for yourselves that they received the same prophecy. However, because Levi represents the spirit, he was chosen to represent the Levitical priest line. Simeon and Levi were the sons of Leah.

In Genesis 34, when Shechem defiled their sister Dinah they tricked Shechem, his father Hamor, and his brothers to become circumcised in order to be married to their sister and the other daughters of Israel.

*"And the sons of Jacob answered Shechem and Hamor his father deceitfully, and said, because he had defiled Dinah their sister:*

*And they said unto them, we cannot do this thing, to give our sister to one that is uncircumcised; for that were a reproach to us:*

*But in this will we consent unto you: if ye will be as we be, that every male of you be circumcised;*

*Then will we give our daughters unto you, and we will take your daughters to us, and we will dwell with you, and we will become one people." (Genesis34:13-16)*

After the men were circumcised and were sore, Simeon and Levi killed every one of them. In Genesis 49:5, their father referred to them as instruments of cruelty.

*"And unto Hamor and unto Shechem his son hearkened all that went out of the gate of his city; and every male was circumcised, all that went out of the gate of his city.*

*And it came to pass on the third day, when they were sore, that two of the sons of Jacob, Simeon and Levi, Dinah's brethren, took each man his sword, and came upon the city boldly, and slew all the males.*

*And they slew Hamor and Shechem his son with the edge of the sword, and took Dinah out of Shechem's house, and went out."*
*(Genesis 34:24-26)*

While it is true that Shechem was wrong and had truly defiled Dinah, Simeon and Levi were labeled instrument of cruelty because they deceived Shechem, his father, and his brothers. They allowed them to become circumcised then killed them. To have them circumcised brought them under a blood covenant and all its benefits.

Bringing them under the blood covenant and then killing them, made this a very cruel act.

When Joshua sent out the spies to Jericho they were hidden by Rahab the harlot. After she and her father and brothers were rescued and brought to the camp of Israel, her father and brothers had to stay outside the camp until such time as they were circumcised.

*"But Joshua had said unto the two men that had spied out the country, go into the harlot's house and bring out thence the woman, and all that she hath, as ye sware unto her.*

*And the young men that were spies went in, and brought out Rahab, and her father, and her mother, and her brethren, and all that she had; and they brought out all her kindred, and left them without the camp of Israel.*

*And they burnt the city with fire, and all that was therein: only the silver, and the gold, and the vessels of brass and of iron, they put into the treasury of the house of the Lord.*

*And Joshua saved Rahab the harlot alive, and her father's household, and all that she had; and she dwelleth in Israel even unto this day; because she hid the messengers, which Joshua sent to spy out Jericho." (Joshua 6:22-25)*

In the book of **Exodus 12:38,** a mixed multitude left Egypt with Moses and the children of Israel. This happened because God said He was going to pass over the house and when He saw the blood everyone inside would be safe.

This is what Simeon and Levi allowed the men from Shechem to do: get under a blood covering and then killed them.

Every thing that we do will be tried by fire. If it is done in the flesh it will burn, but if it is done in the Spirit, we will receive a reward.

*"For other foundation can no man lay than is laid, which is Jesus Christ.*

*Now if any man build upon this foundation of gold, silver, precious stones, wood, hay, stubble;*

*Every man's work shall be made manifest: for the day shall declare it, because it shall be revealed by fire; and the fire shall try every man's work of what sort it is.*

*If any man's work abide which he hath built thereupon, he shall receive a reward.*

*If any man's work shall be burned, he shall suffer loss: but he himself shall be saved; yet so as by fire.*

*Know ye not that ye are the temple of God, and that the Spirit of God dwelleth in you?*

*If any man defile the temple of God, him shall God destroy; for the temple of God is holy, which temple ye are." (1Corinthians 3:11-17)*

In the tabernacle that Moses built, God set out seven steps to get to the Holy of Holiest. The Holy of Holiest is the place where we meet with God; this is called the third dimension.

God has set a pattern for the tabernacle, and two major flesh tests all the way through.

The gate is the entrance to the Tabernacle. We are told to enter His Gates with thanksgiving in our hearts (Psalms100:4). This is the place where we receive salvation.

Once we enter the Tabernacle the first piece of furniture that we will meet is the altar of sacrifice. After salvation we begin the death process, which must take place at the altar of sacrifice.

I believe this altar is the place where the believer must die to fleshly sins that are physically committed, such as in Galatians 5:19-21

*"Now the works of the flesh are manifest, which are these: Adultery, fornication, uncleanness, lasciviousness, idolatry, witch-craft, hatred, variance, emulations, wrath, strife, seditions, here-sies, envying, murders, drunkenness, revellings, and such like; of the which I tell you before, as I have also told you in time past, that they which do such things shall not inherit the Kingdom of God."(Galatians 5:19-21)*

The believer must die to all works of the flesh before they can move on in God. This is where we bury ourselves and erect a tomb stone with the inscription: "There lie the remains of Mary Jean." We must walk away from ourselves no matter how much it hurts. This is the only way that we are going to be able to find the will of God for our lives.

The next piece of furniture is the Laver. This piece looks like a saucer that is filled with water. Water is used for the washing of the hands after the priest completes the sacrifice. The washing of water represents the washing by the word.

King David referred to this as the washing with the word. *"Wherewithal shall a young man cleanse his way? By taking heed thereto according to thy word." (Psalms 119:9)*

After the laver is a door to the Holy Place. This door has five pillars, but not much attention has been paid to it. The focus has been placed on the menorah or seven golden candle sticks, the table of shewbread, the altar of incense, the veil, and the Ark of the Covenant.

These were all considered furniture to complete the seven steps into the tabernacle. There is nothing wrong with this, and I believe that we do need seven steps to get into the Tabernacle. However, there are no accidents in God and there is a reason for everything that he has done.

When God asked Moses to build a Tabernacle and put five pillars at the door to the Holy Place, He had a purpose for this. The five pillars at the entrance to the Holy Place will prepare us for the second flesh test. The door to the Holy Place points to the five fold ministries of the church as recorded in the book of Ephesians.

*"Wherefore He saith, when He ascended up on high, He led captivity captive, and gave gifts unto men.*

*"Now that He ascended, what is it but that He also descended first into the lower parts of the earth?*

*He that descended is the same also that ascended up far above all Heavens, that He might fill all things.*

*And He gave some, apostles; and some, prophets; and some, evangelists; and some, pastors and teachers." (Ephesians 4:8-11)*

I believe that we must go through two flesh tests to get to where God is speaking in the Holy of Holies or the third dimension. The outer court represents the first dimension, the inner court represents the second dimension, and behind the veil represents the third dimension.

The outer court is all man (flesh). The inner court is man and God, and behind the veil or the Holy of Holies is all God.

The first, second, and third dimensions also demonstrated the pattern and the activities of the first three kings of Israel.

King Saul represented the outer court or all man. This is where the priest sacrificed the animal in the open. He killed the animal and took its blood and went into the Holy Place.

King David represented the second dimension or man and God.

In the Holy Place, the priest continues to apply the blood on the pieces of furniture. When he lights the lamp it brings illumination or revelation, which only comes from God.

When he sprinkles the shewbread with incense it speaks of revelation of the word, which causes persecutions. This is ordered by God for our processing.

In **Exodus 25:6,** God instructed Moses to tell the people to bring sweet incense. Incense speaks of trials, but no one calls their trials sweet. When the incense is burned on the altar of incense, it speaks of burning our trials. This can only be done by continuous worship. This is the reason why the apostle Paul writes in **1Thessalonians 5:16-18** *"Rejoice evermore. Pray without ceasing.*

*In every thing give thanks: for this is the will of God in Christ Jesus concerning you."*

The apostle Paul again writes to the Roman saints in **Romans 8:35-39** *"Who shall separate us from the love of Christ? Shall tribulation, or distress, or persecution, or famine, or nakedness, or peril, or sword?*

*As it is written, for thy sake we are killed all the day long; we are accounted as sheep for the slaughter.*

*Nay, in all these things we are more than conquerors through Him that loved us.*

*For I am persuaded, that neither death, nor life, nor angels, nor principalities, nor powers, nor things present, nor things to come,*

*Nor height, nor depth, nor any other creature, shall be able to separate us from the love of God, which is in Christ Jesus our Lord."*

In the mount, God showed Moses that titles or positions given to officers in the church are given at the second door, yet no flesh can come into the Holy of Holies. This is the reason why so many do not get the revelation of what God is saying about His word now.

In the third dimension, God never stops talking. This is the reason Jesus said that man shall not live by bread alone, but by every word that is proceeding out of the mouth of God.

In the Bible, the word Bread represents the Word. Jesus said in **St. John 6:48, "I am the bread of life."**

He also said that He was the manna that the Children of Israel ate in the wilderness. Therefore, when Jesus said that man shall not live by bread alone He was saying that man shall not live by the written word alone, but by the revelation that is coming out of the mouth of God concerning that written word.

Once you get into the third dimension, there is a new revelation that God gives on the same old word that was written.

In **St. Matthew 27,** immediately after Jesus died the veil of the temple was rent from the top to the bottom. One of the reasons the Bible recorded "rented from top to bottom" is to show us that when you come into the presence of the Lord, you must come with your head off. He does not ask for your opinion or your logic. God does all the talking, and we do all the listening.

This is the spot that causes many preachers to fail. Here we have operated in the apostle, the prophet, the pastor, the evangelist and the teacher's office. We got revelation (menorah or light from the candlestick), revelation with persecution (shewbread sprinkled with incense), learn to worship after many trials (altar of incense burning.) After the altar of incense, we must produce enough worship for the veil to be opened so we can go into the presence of God.

Here is where the second flesh test is taken. Your office was given to you to be a servant to the people and to work in the sanctuary or the Holy Place.

The priest had to sprinkle every piece of furniture with the blood of the animal that was sacrificed at the outer court or at the altar of sacrifice. The blood had to be taken from the altar of sacrifice to the Holy of Holies.

*"Having therefore, brethren, boldness to enter into the holiest by the blood of Jesus." (Hebrews 10:19)*

This verse of Scripture tells us that the only way we can enter into the Holy of Holies is by the blood of Jesus. The reason so many fail the second flesh test is that they allow their titles to get to them. They forget that it is all because of the blood of Jesus.

We are never addressed by our position in the presence of Jehovah. He is the only authority, the only majesty, the only sovereignty, and the only Lord and King.

This must be clearly recognized and demonstrated as David did when he was bringing the Ark of the Covenant home. He took off his kingly robe, kept on the ephod, and danced before the Lord because the presence of the Lord had returned to Israel. He demonstrated that he could not be king in the presence of the King.

When the five fold ministry of the church of our Lord and Savior Jesus Christ demonstrates this principal, we will be able to get into the presence of God much easier and really be the voice of God to the people. We will not speak what we feel or think, and in some cases, what we researched.

According to the apostle Paul, He admonished his spiritual son Timothy in **2 Timothy 2:15** *"Study to shew thyself approved unto God, a workman that needeth not to be ashamed, rightly dividing the word of truth."*

He further instructed him to shun profane and vain babblings. He warned that they will increase unto more ungodliness.

This is where we must be very careful. Even though we are to study God's word, we must have a motive and ask the Holy Spirit to teach us and to bring to our remembrance the things that God would have us say for a given occasion.

We would be remiss if we do not recognize that God has given each person natural abilities. If we understand they were given to bring glory to God and no matter how good we are to ourselves, it is still only by the blood of Jesus that we can enter into the presence of the Lord.

If we surrender our natural abilities to the service of the Lord, the Holy Spirit would make them supernatural gifts and talents, and utilize them in the Kingdom of God for the glory of God.

This was so important for the children of Israel in the wilderness. This was the only way they knew which direction to take. It is also applicable for the direction of our churches today.

The priest had to sanctify himself before he began the services in the temple. If he had entered into the presence of the Lord with sin in his life, not only was he killed, but the people would not have heard from God. They would not have known what direction to follow.

This is the reason that a rope was tied around the priest. If and when the bell stops ringing the people knew that the priest was dead. They could not go into the presence of God to take him out or else they would have been killed also. They had to pull him out by the rope.

Let me remind you that it does not matter how much we grow spiritually, we still cannot enter into or stand in the presence of the Lord without the blood of Jesus. We must remember that our actions are weighed.

After Hanna had given birth to Samuel, she concluded that our motives for the things we do are examined by God.

*"Talk no more so exceeding proudly; let not arrogancy come out of your mouth: for the Lord is a God of knowledge, and by Him actions are weighed." (1 Samuel 2:3)*

Hanna was barren and she experienced serious bouts of depression whenever her husband's second wife Peninnah bore him children.

Hannah said many prayers and had different reasons why she wanted a child. One reason was she did not feel loved because she was unable to have children, and she wanted a child because her husband's second wife was having children. Whatever reasons Hannah gave, God did not grant her request for a son until He heard her say she would give the child back to Him.

This is the reason why the fivefold ministry was given to the church to flow in the Kingdom of God, and for the glory of God. Everything God gives us is for His glory. If we seek His Kingdom first, then things will be added; so we need not seek things, just seek the King and His righteousness.

Most people believe they will have to wait to get to Heaven before their works are tried. This seems to be the ultimate judgment for receiving rewards. I believe that our works are being tried now in everything that we do for Christ.

*"And when He had opened the fifth seal, I saw under the altar the souls of them that were slain for the word of God, and for the testimony which they held:*

*And they cried with a loud voice, saying, How long O lord, Holy and true, dost thou not judge and avenge our blood on them that dwell on the earth?*

*And white robes were given unto every one of them; and it was said unto them, that they should rest yet for a little season, until their fellow servants also and their brethren, that should be killed as they were, should be fulfilled." (Revelation 6:9-11)*

Here we see the apostle John describing the souls of the saints slain under the Altar in the Tabernacle. Most activities occur in this Heavenly Tabernacle before the saints are allowed to meet with God in His Holy Mountain.

# CHAPTER THIRTEEN

# THE LAST HIGH PRIEST THE RESURRECTED LORD

Mary Magdalene saw Jesus Christ after He was resurrected and He looked different. She was walking around with Jesus Christ for two and a half years and yet did not recognize Him.

*"And it came to pass afterward that He went throughout every city and village, preaching and shewing the glad tidings of the kingdom of God: and the twelve were with Him,*
*And certain women who had been healed of evil spirits and infirmities, Mary Magdalene, out of whom went seven devils,*
*And Joanna the wife of Chuza, Herod's steward, and Susanna, and many others, which ministered unto Him of their substance."*
*(Luke 8:1-3)*

Mary Magdalene supported Jesus Christ wherever He went. She knew what He looked liked but had not seen Him for three days. There had to be some drastic changes in Jesus Christ. She saw a resurrected Christ with a resurrected body.

John saw Christ on the Isle of Patmos with a resurrected body. He saw a man with white hair like lamb's wool. Christ came out of the grave with his resurrected body. His body went through shock so Mary did not recognize him.

Doctors believe when the body goes through shock or trauma it turns grey.

Jesus Christ's body was marred. Isaiah said there was no beauty that could be desired of Him. The word marred means His body was sliced and chopped. His body was so marred He was beyond recognition. Jesus Christ had His beard pulled out. His body went through so much that His arteries were severed. Every blood vessel burst. Every drop of blood had to come out of Him.

When Mary saw Him she mistook Him for the gardener. He had on a garment, which wasn't a regular garment. They whipped Him until His flesh was lying in ribbons. He was accused of blaspheming God. The penalty for blasphemy was to first pour hot lead then dung down the throat, and then throw the person in a place of muck and mire called Ghenna. The punishment involved dropping the victim in Ghenna or burning them at the stake until there were no remains.

This is the reason the Bible told us that Joseph of Arimathea begged for the body of Jesus. Pilate had another plan for the body of Jesus and that was to throw it in Ghenna.

The clothes Jesus was wrapped in were left in the grave after He was resurrected, but when Mary Magdalene saw Him, He looked like the gardener. He told Mary Magdalene not to touch Him, and then He went to Heaven.

I believe that since He was the last High Priest, He had on the High Priest robe when He went into Heaven and sprinkled the furniture in the Tabernacle in Heaven with His own blood.

I also believe when Jesus was resurrected, the Holy Spirit brought the original High Priest's robe from Heaven and dressed Jesus in it. Moses patterned Aaron and his sons robe just like this one.

In **Genesis 14:18-20,** *"And Melchizedek King of Salem brought forth bread and wine: and he was the priest of the most High God.*

*And he blessed him, and said blessed be Abram of the most High God, possessor of Heaven and earth.*

*And blessed be the Most High God, which hath delivered thine enemies into thy hand. And he gave him tithes of all."*

Melchizedek had no record of father or mother birth or death. His genealogy was not counted; therefore, he could be a type of

Jesus Christ who had no earthly father or mother in birth or death. Jesus Christ was a Divine Being.

*"For unto us a child is born, unto us a Son is given: and the government shall be upon His shoulder: and His name shall be called Wonderful, Counsellor, The Mighty God, The Everlasting Father, The Prince of Peace." (Isaiah 9:6)*

*"But thou Bethlehem Ephratah, though thou be little among the thousands of Judah, yet out of thee shall He come forth unto me that is to be ruler in Israel; Whose goings forth have been from of old, from everlasting." (Micah 5:2)*

*"In the beginning was the Word, and the Word was with God, and the Word was God. The same was in the beginning with God." (St. John 1:1-2)*

*"But unto the Son He saith, Thy throne O God is forever and ever: A scepter of Righteousness is the scepter of Thy Kingdom." (Hebrew 1:8)*

*"I am Alpha and Omega, the Beginning and the ending, saith the Lord, which is, and which was, and which is to come, the Almighty.*

*I John who also am your brother, and companion in tribulation, and in the Kingdom and patience of Jesus Christ, was in the Isles that is call Patmos, for the testimony of Jesus Christ.*

*I was in the Spirit on the Lord's Day, and heard behind me a great voice, as of a trumpet,*

*Saying I am Alpha and Omega, the First and the Last: and what thou seest, write in a book, and send it unto the seven churches in Asia; unto Ephesus, and unto Smyrna, and unto Pergamos, and unto Thyatira, and unto Sardis, and unto Philadelphia, and unto Laodicea." (Revelation 1:8-11)*

As God, Christ was not begotten, He was not God's Son, and He had no birth or death. Only as man did the second person of the Divine Trinity have a begetting: a father, a mother, a birth and a death.

*"And we declare unto you glad tidings, how that the promise which was made unto the fathers,*

*God hath fulfilled the same unto us their children, in that He hath raised up Jesus again; as it also written in the second psalm. Thou art my Son, This day have I begotten thee." (Acts 13:32-33)*

*Psalms 2:7, "I will declare the degree: the Lord hath said unto me, Thou art my Son: this day have I begotten thee."*

Jesus Christ was the seed of Abraham, but His priest line is not of the Levitical line. Abraham paid tithes into the priest line that Jesus Christ was coming through. This is the eternal priest line.

*"For this Melchizedek, King of Salem, Priest of the Most High God, who met Abraham returning from the slaughter of the Kings, and blessed him;*

*To whom also Abraham gave a tenth part of all; first being by interpretation King of righteousness, and after that also King of Salem, which is, King of Peace.*

*Without father, without mother, without descent, having neither beginning of days, nor end of life; but made like unto the Son of God, abideth a priest continually.*

*Now consider how great this man was, unto whom even the patriarch Abraham gave the tenth of the spoils.*

*And verily they that are of the sons of Levi, who receive the office of the priesthood, have a commandment to take tithes of the people according to the law, that is, of their brethren, though they came out of the loins of Abraham:*

*But he whose descent is not counted from them received tithes of Abraham, and blessed him that had the promises.*

*And without all contradiction the less is blessed of the better.*

*And here men that die receive tithes; but there He receiveth them, of whom it is witnessed that He liveth.*

*And as I may so say, Levi also, who receiveth tithes, paid tithes in Abraham.*

*For he was yet in the loins of his father, when Melchizedek met him.*

*If therefore perfection were by the Levitical priesthood, for under it the people received the law, what further need was there that another priest should rise after the order of Melchizedek, and not be called after the order of Aaron?*

*For the priesthood being changed, there is made of necessity a change also of the law.*

*For He of whom these things are spoken pertaineth to another tribe, of which no man gave attendance at the altar.*

*For it is evident that our Lord sprang out of Juda: of which tribe Moses spake nothing concerning priesthood.*

*And it is yet far more evident: for that after the similitude of Melchizedek there ariseth another priest.*

*Who is made not after the law of a carnal commandment, but after the power of an endless life.*

*For he testifieth, Thou art a priest for ever after the order of Melchizedek." Hebrews 7:1-17*

The book of Hebrew states, Jesus Christ is not after the priest line of Aaron and Abraham. According to Genesis, Jesus Christ came through the order of Melchizedek; a priest line established by God for Christ forever.

The temple in Heaven is open.

*"And I turned to see the voice that spake with me. And being turned, I saw seven golden candlesticks;*

*And in the midst of the seven one like unto the son of man, clothed with a garment down to the foot, and girt about the paps with a golden girdle." (Revelation 1:12-13)*

The apostle John sees Christ as a High Priest wearing a golden girdle. This shows that our High Priest is at work in Heaven making intercession for us.

*"His head and his hairs were white like wool, as white as snow; and His eyes were as flame of fire." (Revelation 1:14)*

Jesus head and hairs present Him as Christ the Judge. His eyes as flame of fire portray Him as the Omniscient one: the all-knowing and the all-seeing one.

In the **fifteenth verse of this chapter**, the apostle John records *"And His feet like unto fine brass, as if they burned in a furnace; and His voice as the sound of many waters."* He sees Jesus as the conqueror and the giver of the Holy Spirit.

We have to remember that the apostle John is seeing the resurrected Lord. This is one of the most detailed descriptions of Jesus since He was resurrected. The apostle Paul heard His voice on the road to Damascus, but saw no man.

The apostle John continued to describe his vision of Christ.

In **verse sixteen** he writes, *"And He had in His Right Hand seven stars: and out of His mouth went a sharp two edged sword: and His countenance was as the sun shineth in his strength."*

Here Jesus is seen holding the leaders of the church in the palm of His hand. He is correcting the leaders by praising them for what is right, and pointing out the things that are wrong.

Every leader reading this book should be encouraged to stand for what is true. There are so many who claimed they have a word from the Lord for the leader while they themselves are not in submission to their leader.

This is the order that God will follow for the preparation and perfection of the last day church. He will correct His leaders, and the leaders will correct the churches. Any one taking correction from someone that is not in authority in the church, especially if the person is in opposition to the leader, that person is in rebellion.

Correction from the leader that has been corrected by God is direction. This is very important for persons who want to be a part of God's last day church. What does this mean? God is going to correct His leaders, not a board, and God's leaders will correct the board and the membership.

The last part of verse sixteen, John saw Jesus' countenance as the sun shining in its strength. This speaks of Jesus being the expressed image of the Father.

This is just a reminder that Jesus Christ is the **"I Am."** After His resurrection, He is in the many offices that He holds and is letting the leaders of the churches know that He would be any one that they needed, and that He would help them and their congregation get ready for the rapture.

This is why I believe that Jesus' eternal name is **"I AM."** The eternal priest line was, and is, and ever more shall be in Him.

# FULL COVERING IN ONE HIGH PRIEST

lucifer had a robe that was similar to the High Priest, and his covering had the same precious stones that were on the robe the High Priest wore. However, his covering only had nine stones, while the robe that God told Moses to make for the High Priest had twelve. This High Priest's robe was made after a replica of the High Priest's Robe in Heaven.

The High Priest's robe had twelve precious stones: four rows, with three stones in each row. lucifer's covering had only three rows with three stones each; he was missing an entire row with three stones. The three precious stones that were missing were from the tribe of the children of Israel. They were Issachar, Gad and Asher.

For us to understand why these three stones were missing from lucifer's covering, we have to revisit **Genesis 49;** where Jacob spoke the meaning of his children names and predicted their future.

We must also remember that whatever office a person holds, the covering or anointing was given for it. An example of this is found in the story of Miriam and Aaron rebellion against Moses for marrying an Ethiopian woman.

God called Moses, Aaron, and Miriam to the tabernacle of the congregation. God stood in the door of the tabernacle and asked Aaron and Miriam to step forth. God reprimanded them for coming against Moses His leader. Miriam became leprous; Aaron did not.

God told Moses to make Aaron a priest. While Aaron was standing before the Tabernacle he had on his priestly robe. The priest's robe represents the anointing or the covering for Aaron's office.

Even though Miriam may have played a tambourine and danced on many occasions, there is no place in the Scriptures where God told Moses to anoint her for a position. Her only covering was Moses and she was coming against him.

When it was time for Aaron to die, God told Moses to take his robe off him and put it on another generation. Moses did this and Aaron died.

This was also the main reason why David's heart smote him when he clipped the cloak of King Saul. He knew that Saul was anointed and that his cloak represented the covering or the anointing for the office he held.

I hope you see the importance of why God left certain stone off lucifer's covering.

*"Issachar is a strong ass crouching down between two burdens:*

*And he saw that rest was good, and the land that it was pleasant; and bowed his shoulder to bear, and became a servant unto tribute." (Genesis 49:14-15)*

Here Issachar is described as helping to bear burdens. This stone was missing from lucifer's covering, because he will never be a burden bearer or help to bear burdens.

*"Gad, a troop shall overcome him: but he shall overcome at last." (Genesis 49:19)*

Here it is said that no matter what happen to Gad, one day he will overcome. No matter what goes on in your life: past, present or future, satan will never help you to overcome; nor will he ever overcome himself.

*"Out of Asher, his bread shall be fat, and he shall yield royal dainties." (Genesis 49:20)*

This verse states that Asher represents royalty. This stone was missing from lucifer's covering because there has never been and never will be anything royal about the devil.

Now you can examine **Ezekiel 28:13** to see the listing of precious stones in lucifer's covering, and which three were missing.

According to this passage of Scripture, satan wanted to be high priest. During the tribulation, he will possess the antichrist and will go into the temple in Jerusalem and defile it; still trying to become a high priest.

*"How art thou fallen from Heaven, O lucifer, son of the morning! How art thou cut down to the ground, which didst weaken the nations!*

*For thou hast said in thine heart, I will ascend into Heaven, I will exalt my throne above the stars of God I will sit also upon the mount of the congregation, in the sides of the north." (Isaiah 14:12-13)*

The tabernacle of God is located just before the mountain of God. This tabernacle is where the congregation of Heaven passes through to get to the holy mountain of God for worship. Every tabernacle must have a priest. Because lucifer led the praise and had to go through this tabernacle to get to the mountain of God, he thought that he was the High Priest of Heaven. Heaven has its own High Priest and He is sitting at the right hand of the Father.

Every priest on the earth had to take blood into the tabernacle. lucifer took his rebellion into Heaven, and messed up the place in the tabernacle where the congregation of Heaven passed through to get to the holy mountain of God. This is the place where all of our works will be tried.

According to *1 Corinthians 3:13-15, "Every man's work shall be made manifest: for the day shall declare it, because it shall be revealed by fire; and the fire shall try every man's work of what sort it is.*

*If any man's work abide which he had built thereupon, he shall receive a reward.*

*If any man's work shall be burned, he shall suffer loss: but he himself shall be saved; yet so as by fire."*

This is also the place that Jesus went to prepare for us according to **St. John 14:2-3.** *"In my Father's house are many mansions: if it were not so, I would have told you. I go to prepare a place for you.*

*And if I go and prepare a place for you, I will come again, and receive you unto myself; that where I am, there ye may be also."*

As I said before, lucifer took his rebellion into Heaven and messed the place up; so when Jesus said that He went to prepare a place for us, He actually went to fix the place that lucifer messed up with sin.

The high priest that worked the tabernacle on earth had to go into the tabernacle, and sprinkled all the furniture with the blood from an animal that was sacrificed in the outer court.

*"For ever, O Lord Thy word is settled in Heaven." (Psalms 119:89)*

This is the reason why God did not received Cain's offering. God had already settled in Himself that without the shedding of blood there would be no remission for sin. Throughout this book, I have presented the facts, as a lawyer would in a court case, to reinforce the power that is in the blood of Jesus.

We may be convinced at this time that every one on earth needed the blood of Jesus. We need a redeemer, and we need the blood of Jesus for many other reasons. Whatever God says is final and He never goes against His word.

*"I will worship toward Thy holy temple, and praise Thy name for thy loving kindness and for thy truth: for thou hast magnified Thy word above all Thy name." (Psalms 138:2)*

We explained how important the blood of Christ is for everyone on the earth, but what does His blood have to do with Heaven? The place that lucifer messed up in Heaven needed blood for cleansing. God looked around in Heaven and saw no one with blood. All angels are spirit beings, including lucifer.

When Jesus died on the cross, His blood was not only shed to wash away our sins, but also to cleanse Heaven and to fix the place that lucifer messed up.

*"But Christ being an High Priest of good things to come, by a greater and more perfect tabernacle, not made with hands that is to say, not of this building;*

*Neither by the blood of goats and calves, but by His own blood He entered in once into the holy place, having obtained eternal redemption for us." (Hebrews 9:11-12)*

*"Moreover the word of the Lord came unto me, saying, Son of man, take up a lamentation upon the king of Tyrus, and say unto him, thus saith the Lord God: Thou sealest up the sum, full of wisdom, and perfect in beauty. Thou*

*had been in Eden, the garden of God; every precious stone was thy covering. The sardius, topaz, and the diamond, the beryl, the onyx, and the jasper, the sapphire, the emerald, and the carbuncle, and gold: the workmanship of thy tabrets and of thy pipes was prepared in thee in the day that thou wast created. Thou art the anointed cherub that covereth: and I have set thee so: thou wast upon the Holy mountain of God; thou hast walked up and down in the midst of the stones of fire. Thou wast perfect in thy ways from the day that thou wast created, till iniquity was found in thee. By the multitude of thy merchandise they have filled the midst of thee with violence, and thou hast sinned: therefore I will cast thee as profane out of the mountain of God; and I will destroy thee O covering cherub, from the midst of the stones of fire. Thine heart was lifted up because of thy beauty; thou hast corrupted thy wisdom by reason of thy brightness: I will cast thee to the ground; I will lay thee before kings, that they may behold thee. Thou hast defiled thy sanctuaries by the multitude of thine iniquities, by the iniquity of thy traffick; therefore will I bring forth a fire from the midst of thee, it shall devour thee, and I will I bring thee to ashes upon the earth in the sight of all them that behold thee. All they that know thee among the people shall be astonished at thee: thou shalt be a terror, and never shalt thou be any more." (Ezekiel 28:11-19)*

God smeared the anointing on lucifer. He was in charge of praise and worship. We cannot enter God's presence unless we offer worship. In order to go through the temple door of the tabernacle, acceptable worship had to be presented.

satan led the angels of God through this temple for worship. He was the praise leader. Since his robe was missing three stones, he was never complete, so he defiled the holy place when he rebelled against God. After satan was kicked out of Heaven, he decided to go up to the holy place but God denied him access into the temple. The Bible said he covered the throne of God and the glory of God shone through him.

Even though satan had on something similar to the priest's garment, it was not complete. The priestly garment was reserved for the only begotten Son of God.

It was Gabriel who stood in God's presence and delivered His messages to the people. It was Michael, the warrior of Heaven, who was sent from God's presence to go and fight.

satan was an archangel and was next in line to the Godhead.

It was lucifer who led the angels in praise and worship and into the presence of God. His robe was not completed, so he would never be able to help people or bear their burdens.

# CHAPTER FOURTEEN

# THE FIRST AND SECOND ADAM

This is like man today; man thinks he is so great and intelligent. Men think they can create another human being. Scientists have already cloned animals and invented human beings through artificial insemination. They can make mannequins that look like man, and get them to move with the use of batteries, electricity and computers, but they can't breathed into man and make him a living soul.

God breathed into Adam's nostrils and he became a living soul and blood flowed through his veins. Ever since this happened, we know that the life of the flesh is in the blood, **(Leviticus 17:11.)** Adam lie down in the dust and when God breathe into him His breath, then blood came.

Every time I approach the Bible, I allow God to be the all knowing one and I the limited one. If there are some things that I don't understand, I don't accuse God of not knowing what He is doing or that He made a mistake or that He is contradicting Himself. Instead, I realized that I am the one that have not received the revelation of what He is saying or what He is doing.

Having said all that, there are many questions in my mind concerning the blood of Jesus. Since there is no one with blood in heaven, the question is where did all this blood come from: the fish of the sea, the fowls of the air, and the blood in the first Adam?

As the life of the flesh is in the blood and it was God who gave life to both man and animals, we can now see why in the beginning both man and animals were at peace in the Garden of Eden.

*"And God said, let us make man in our image, and after our likeness: and let them have dominion over the fish of the sea, and over the fowl of the air, and over the cattle, and over all the earth, and over every creeping thing that creepeth upon the earth." (Genesis 1:26)*

I believe that the blood in animals is different from the blood in man. In **Psalms 8,** God said that He made man a little lower than angels. I believe He made the animals lower than man. It was only when God was creating man that He said, lets us make man in our image and after our likeness. The image of God came from the dust, but the likeness of God came from the blood.

When God breathed into man, man became a living soul. The soul is the intellect, the way we think. This is the reason why when God brought the animals for Adam to name; whatever Adam called them God agreed with Him. Before Adam sinned or contaminated the blood his thoughts were like God's because God was his only teacher.

Both the first Adam and the second Adam had the same Father. The first Adam started out as an adult male, but the second Adam started out as a seed. It would appear that the second Adam started out as a seed so that He would test every stage that we would go through in life.

*"And so it is written, the first man Adam was made a living soul: the last Adam was made a quickening Spirit. Howbeit that was not first which was spiritual, but that which is natural; and afterward that which is spiritual. The first man is of the earth, earthy: the second man is the Lord from Heaven. As is the earthy, such are they also that are earthy: and as is the heavenly, such are they also that are heavenly. And as we have borne the image of the earthy, we shall also bear the image of the heavenly. Now this I say,*

**brethren that flesh and blood cannot inherit the kingdom of God: neither doth corruption inherit incorruption." (1 Corinthians 15:45-50)**

It is clear from this passage of Scripture that the first Adam produces only physical seed and the second Adam produces only spiritual seeds. We cannot become one without the other, and the physical comes first then the spiritual.

The first Adam was formed from the physical earth, while the second Adam came from Heaven as a seed. The laws of God have always been settled in Heaven. One of these laws is that each seed will produce after its kind. This makes it crystal clear that all persons in the earth are physical seed of the first Adam; and every one that becomes born again are the spiritual seed of the second Adam, Jesus Christ. This makes us joint heirs with Him. For every wise man leaves an inheritance of what he has, and what he is, to his children and to his children's children.

Once we are born into this world, we are the physical descendants of the first Adam; and once we are Christians, we are the spiritual descendants of the Second Adam.

If a child is born with any of its members missing from its body, we call him or her a deformed child. If a person happens to have a member of its body lost or amputated, we say that he or she is handicapped. All of this is said because our physical bodies are always compared to the original body that God made for Adam.

After the first Adam sinned, we also inherited the effects of sin, sickness, pains, heartaches, disappointments, confusion, betrayal, death, and the list goes on all because of being the physical seed of the first Adam.

Every one of the conditions listed, and more, have been experienced by the physical seed of the first Adam. Someone somewhere can relate to these experiences from the first Adam. What about the second Adam and His seed inheritance? The spiritual Adam became flesh and dwelled among us.

*"And the Word was made flesh, and dwelt among us, and we beheld His glory, the glory as of the only begotten of the Father, full of Grace and Truth." (St. John 1:14)*

Here we see the spiritual Adam becoming flesh and living among men. The sin of the first Adam brought curses on the entire human race. God sent the Second Adam to become flesh and to die on the cross so the curses that came because of the first Adam's sin could be destroyed from the entire human race. After the Second Adam died the curses of the human race were destroyed.

*"Christ had redeemed us from the curse of the law, being made a curse for us: For it is written, Cursed is every one that hangeth on a tree: That the blessings of Abraham might come on the gentiles through Jesus Christ; that we might receive the promise of the Spirit through faith." (Galatians 3:13-14)*

Just as every member of our physical body has to be whole, there are benefits that we receive when the spiritual Adam died.

*"Surely He had borne our griefs, and carried our sorrows: yet we did esteem Him stricken, smitten of God, and afflicted. But He was wounded for our transgressions, bruised for our iniquities: the chastisement of our peace was upon Him: and with His stripes we are healed." (Isaiah 53:4-5)*

Because of the death of the Second Adam, we are promised complete healing of our bodies.

The tenth verse of this chapter puts it even clearer.

*"Yet it please the Lord to bruise Him He had put Him to grief: when thou shalt make His soul an offering for sin, He shall see His seed, He shall prolong His days, and the pleasure of the Lord shall prosper in His hand." (Isaiah 53:10)*

Did you notice in the tenth verse that Jesus has a seed and He will see His seed? Recently, on an Easter Sunday morning, God asked me to sow a seed. He told me that if I would sow my best seed, I would receive a harvest from this seed similar to the harvest He is receiving from the grain of corn He sowed over two thousand years ago. God reminded me that the grain of corn He sowed has never stopped giving Him a harvest.

Every time you hear of someone receiving Jesus Christ as Saviour and Lord, the harvest is continuing. This is one of the benefits that you get from the second Adam.

*"Many are the afflictions of the righteous, but the Lord delivereth him out of them all." (Psalms 34:19)*

This passage of Scripture promised deliverance for every believer. This deliverance is not for Heaven, it is for this present earth and it has been accomplished through the second Adam.

*"He that committed sin is of the devil; for the devil sinneth from the beginning. For this purpose the Son of God was manifested, that He might destroy the works of the devil." (1 John 3:8)*

When Jesus died on the cross of Calvary and was buried and resurrected, He destroyed the works of the devil. He declared that all power was given unto Him. He gave us that same power over all the works of the devil so that we can enjoy all the benefits of the Second Adam.

Scientific facts prove that children have something in them that helps their body to heal itself. If a child is cut or scarred he heals much faster than adults. As a child gets older, and an x-tray is taken of the cut or scar it will show that the scars or marks have disappeared. It is believed that this started with Adam because God had intended for Adam to live forever.

In the back of a human head, near the brain, is a closed spot. When a baby is born this spot is opened. This spot is there to help the child receive knowledge. Unfortunately, because of sin, when the child gets to a certain age this spot closes.

God never intended for Adam to go to school or have knowledge from the world. God was his teacher. Adam was smarter than any human being in the world today. There was an opening in Adam's brain that gave God access to him; that is why God did not want him to eat of the tree of good and evil. The tree would have introduced him to the world system. Man sinned and became limited.

If it were possible to obtain an autopsy of God the father and match it to the blood of Jesus Christ the Son, it would be proven that their blood are the same. When God dispatched the seed and placed it in Mary, the blood of God the Father was in that seed. All children have their father's blood.

## ALL TEMPLE FURNITURE ARE SPRINKLED WITH BLOOD

The temple in Heaven needed blood. There was a golden altar in the temple. Under this altar were the souls of the saints that were slain. Those are the tribulation saints whose blood will cry out for revenge. Their blood will be symbolic of the blood of Jesus. Their blood will be avenged when the wrath of God is poured upon the earth. God wants to give us a fresh look at the power of the blood. Both the Old and New Testaments were dedicated with blood.

When God told Moses to build a tabernacle after the pattern that He had shown him in the mountain, He was not only talking about the physical appearance of the tabernacle, but also the inner activities of the tabernacle.

*"Whereupon neither the first Testament was dedicated without blood. For when Moses had spoken every precept to all the people according to the law, he took the blood of calves and of goats, with water, and scarlet wool, and hyssop, and sprinkled both the book and all the people, saying, this is the blood of the Testament which God had enjoined unto you. Moreover he sprinkled with blood both the tabernacle and all the vessels of the ministry. And almost all things*

*are by law purged with blood; and without the shedding of blood is no remission. (Hebrews 9:18-22)*

Moses went into the tabernacle and the first thing he did was sprinkle the four horns of the altar with blood. He then goes to the laver that looks like a basin and sprinkle it with blood. He sprinkled the seven candlesticks with blood. Then he goes to the table with the shew bread and sprinkled them with blood. He goes further into the holy place and sees the Ark of the Covenant and sprinkled it with blood. The High Priest had to be sure to clean and sanctify himself for seven days before he went into the Holy of Holies.

We have a High Priest that entered once a year and sprinkled everything that was in the tabernacle with blood.

Jesus Christ our High Priest goes in and meets every instrument of ministry that Moses had. These are in the temple of God in Heaven. The difference between Moses and the Last High Priest is that while Moses and the priest work in a tabernacle on earth, the Last High Priest, Jesus Christ, was sprinkling his blood on the furniture in Heaven. There were different priest orders for example: Zachariah's role was to keep the incense burning. Jesus Christ came through an order that was not of this world.

*"But thou Bethlehem Ephratah, though thou be little among the thousands of Judah, yet out of thee shall he come forth unto me that is to be ruler in Israel; whose goings forth have been from of old, from everlasting." (Micah 5:2)*

God was depending on him to deliver all of mankind from their sins. When Jesus prayed in the garden of Gethsemane, He was not praying not to die when He said,

*"Father, if thou be willing, remove this cup from me: nevertheless not my will, but thine, be done." Luke 22:42*

He knew that dying was the purpose for which He came. Jesus was praying that he would not die before he got to the cross. He could not have a premature death. In **Numbers 21:5**, the children spoke against God and against Moses and said:

*"Wherefore have ye brought us up out of Egypt to die in the wilderness? For there is no bread, neither is there any water; and our soul loatheth this light bread."(Numbers 21:5)*

The Lord sent fiery serpents among the people, and they bit them and many of the children of Israel died. When Israel repented, God told Moses to make a fiery serpent of brass and put it on a pole. All those that were bitten, when they look upon the serpent would live. The children of Israel looked at the serpent and lived.

When Jesus had a discussion with Nicodemus about the Kingdom of God and being born again, He referred to the lifting up of the serpent in the wilderness by Moses. This was a pattern of what had to happen to Him.

*"And as Moses lifted up the serpent in the wilderness, even so must the son of man be lifted up." (St. John 3:14)*

This was the reason He didn't pray not to die, but that He did not die in the garden where He was praying and was about to be arrested by the soldiers. If He had died there, He would have contradicted Himself, because it was already written about Him. Jesus Himself said:

*"And I If I be lifted up from the earth, will draw all men unto me." (St. John 12:32)*
*"For consider Him that endured such contradiction of sinners against Himself, lest ye be wearied and faint in your minds. Ye have not yet resisted unto blood, striving against sin." (Hebrews 12:3– 4)*

Jesus had to fulfil every Scripture that was written concerning Him by the prophets. After He fed the 5,000 they tried to crown Him King. The crowds pushed Him to the edge of the cliff. The devil didn't mind Jesus dying, but not on the cross.

*"Howbeit we speak the wisdom among them that are perfect: Yet not the wisdom of this world, nor of the princes of this world, that come to nought: But we speak the wisdom of God in a mystery, even the hidden wisdom, which God ordained before the world unto our glory: Which none of the princes of this world knew: for had they known it, they would not have crucified the Lord of Glory."(1 Corinthians 2:6-8)*

The mystery of the cross was hidden from the devil and all principalities. When Jesus came from the garden, He set His face like a flint and went toward Jerusalem to face death. He knew He had to die and He knew He had to be lifted up, so He could draw all men unto Him. He had His priestly robe when He returned to Heaven. Every other priest's robe was made after the pattern of His. He is the first and last High Priest of Heaven. All the others are shadows and types of the real High Priest robe. His body and blood were simply incorruptible.

## CHAPTER FIFTEEN

# NEW REVELATION OF GOD

There is one thing that brings you more persecutions, and that is another revelation of God. In order to get another revelation of God you must get a revelation of His word. There are levels in God that we don't know.

*"But call to remembrance the former days, in which, after ye were illuminated, ye endured a great fight of afflictions." (Hebrew 10:32)*

The word illuminate means light or to turn on light. So God is saying after you receive light on the word, persecutions will come. With illumination comes revelation so that you can grow in God. When you receive revelation of God's word, God is giving you a new insight on a word that you did not see the last time you read that same word.

Each new level brings new devils. The demons that came against you were not sent to fight you on your next level. The first time you read the word, it is at a certain level; as you grow you see more in depth, and more of God is revealed. Stronger demons or devils are sent as you move to different levels.

The two men on the way to Emmaus were on different levels. Jesus was in a dimension that the two men on the road to Emmaus were not in.

satan's kingdom also has new levels: principalities, powers, rulers of darkness, and spiritual wickedness in high places.

*"For we wrestle not against flesh and blood, but against principalities, against powers, against the rulers of the darkness of this world, against spiritual wickedness in high places." (Ephesians 6:12)*

To get revelations from God comes with a fight. The more revelation of God you experience the more the enemy will fight you. You can live in such a place in God where the devil will never find you. You can reach to a place in God where you have authority over every devil in hell. The devil was the only angel recorded in the Bible that God anointed and clothed.

*"Thou hast been in Eden the garden of God: every precious stone was thy covering, the sardius, topaz, and the diamond, the beryl, the onyx, and the jasper, the sapphire, the emerald, and the carbuncle, and gold: the workmanship of thy tabrets and of thy pipes was prepared in thee in the day that thou wast created.(Ezekiel 28:14)*

Isaiah saw the Lord high and lifted up in the temple. This temple was in Heaven, and the seraphim were producing glory as they worshipped every new revelation of the Holiness of God.

**Ezekiel 47** shows the different levels of anointing in God. The first 1,000 cubits in God, the water or anointing is ankle deep. The water or anointing gets to the knees in the second level. In the third level the water or anointing gets to the loins; and in the fourth level, the anointing becomes a river you can swim in.

These levels can also be compared to the different categories of demons and principalities the saints encounter as they grow in God.

The blood covenant we have in Christ gives us a privilege Aaron didn't have. If the bells stopped ringing, the congregation would know that the priest was unclean, and they would pull him out of the holy place.

A lot of church people make noise, but have no fruit; the noise and fruit go together.

# THE SCAPEGOAT

Aaron would go in and give three offerings. One of the offerings would be a goat. Goats were raised as pets, so when it was time to sacrifice them, it was painful to let go. They gave up the closest thing to them.

The priest had to cleanse himself for seven days. The elders would question him for four days to be sure he had no sin in his life. For three days the priest had to spend time with God. He had to make sure God accepted him first. He had to be sure his family had no sin, and lived pure lives before God.

Likewise, in families today the man must live as priest and establish an altar in the home.

In **Leviticus 16,** there are several teachings concerning the scape goat. Both goats represent Christ. If a lamb or goat was killed, the priest would sprinkle the Ark of the Covenant with its blood. When the tabernacle was built, the priest would actually sprinkle all the furniture or instruments with the blood of the goat or lamb.

The goat is symbolic of Jesus Christ, the atonement for sin. They could not send a dead goat which symbolized the death of Christ.

Using a living goat, the priest would lay his hands on the goat, confess the sins of the people, and have someone lead the goat out into the wilderness. The person who led the goat out side the camp must be physically fit, so that he can take the goat far away where he could not see civilization. If he was not fit, that person would die before the goat did.

The scapegoat is a symbol of Christ taking our sins away; so far away, as the East is from the West. The goat would be led so far from the camp, that it could not find its way back into the camp.

The same way Christ forgets our sins. Our sins are only remembered when we go back and do them again. The scapegoat is the lamb who was crucified, resurrected, and carried our sins so far away that they are placed in the sea of forgetfulness and are remembered no more. Jesus Christ is our scapegoat.

The scapegoat in the Old Testament went to a land not inhabited. It represented Christ carrying our sins so far away that no one can ever retrieve them again. (No fishing Allowed.)

# CHAPTER SIXTEEN

# THE BLOOD GIVES US ACCESS

*"Having therefore, brethren, boldness to enter into the Holiest by the blood of Jesus." (Hebrews 10:19)*

Y ou cannot approach God without the blood. Some people make requests unto God and say they didn't get an answer. Sometimes they have not gotten into God's presence so they can't get an answer. God's Word cannot lie.

> *"God is not a man, that He should lie; neither the son of man, that He should repent: hath He said, and shall He not do it? Or hath He spoken, and shall He not make it good?" (Numbers 23:19)*
>
> *"That by two immutable things, in which it is impossible for God to lie, we might have a strong consolation, who have fled for refuge to lay hold upon the hope set before us." (Hebrews 6:18)*

This is telling us that we can take refuge in what ever God says. It is impossible for God to lie. We know that He honors His word above His name and that His word cannot return to Him void. God also watches over His word and He hastens to perform His word.

*"And in that day ye shall ask me nothing. Verily, verily, I say unto you, whatsoever ye shall ask the Father in my name, He will give it you." (St. John 16:23)*

God is simply saying, if you come to Me in My Son's name I will not refuse you; I will answer you.

*"But we all, with open face beholding as in a glass the glory of the Lord, are changed into the same image from glory to glory, even as by the Spirit of the Lord." (2 Corinthians 3:18)*

When we go to God, we address him as *"Our Father."* We hallow His name. However, we can't go into God's presence in the flesh. No flesh shall glory in His presence. That's why when Moses asked to see God's glory He actually hid him in the cleft of the rock. God talked to Moses face to face, but He hid him. When Moses came down from the mountain he was a reflection of the glory of God. When the people looked at him they hid their faces.

When Moses spoke to the people he put a veil over his face. He couldn't talk to them face to face until some of the glory from the presence of God, wore off. There's absolutely no one who gets into the presence of God and comes out the same way. There must be change in the presence of God. The presence of God changes your walk, talk and looks.

The Word of God says in **1 John 3:2,** *"Beloved now we are the sons of God and it does not yet appear what we shall be like, but we shall be like Him, we shall see Him as He is."*

We shall be conformed to His image and His likeness. Moses spent time with God and he was transformed.

When Lazarus came out of the grave, he had to be loosed from his grave clothes he was wrapped in. When Jesus came out of the grave He was already loosed. The stone was not rolled away to let Him out, but to allow Mary Magdalene and the disciples to see inside the tomb, for it was the Holy Spirit who resurrected Him.

When Mary Magdalene saw Him, He was wearing a robe. Where did the robe come from? Some people believe He may have gotten it from His mother. That isn't possible because His mother was with His disciples. He told Mary Magdalene not to touch Him because He had not yet visited His Father since coming out of the grave. That evening, He came to His disciples and told Thomas to touch Him. I believe He had already visited the Father.

Light travels at 180,000 miles per second, and it will take years for light to reach the sun and planets. Heaven is further away than the planets. I believe Jesus Christ made the trip in seconds. Mary saw Jesus in the morning, and that same evening He told Thomas to touch him.

Job 38, talks about the dedication of the earth. When the earth was dedicated the corner stone was laid; Jesus was the corner stone. Jesus Christ is the Lamb of God that was slain from the foundation of the world. The Lamb of God died from the foundation of the world, because God knew that both Heaven and Earth would need Jesus' blood for cleansing.

Heaven is in the North, Psalms 75:6 and Isaiah 14:13. Scientist has proven that Heaven is in the North; they have discovered an opening in the sky in the Northern part of the atmosphere. With the exception of this one place, there are stars all over the world. There is an opening that goes straight up, and there are no stars or planets.

The Middle East where all the crisis is taking place today is located in the North. The battle of Armageddon will be fought in the North. The abyss satan will be thrown into is in the North. When Jesus Christ ascended, he went towards the North. lucifer will be converging in the North for his final battle. The New Jerusalem is also coming from the North.

In the Old Testament, once a year on the Day of Atonement the priest entered the tabernacle. The Bible says that Jesus Christ came as a high priest of good things to come by a greater and more perfect tabernacle. Jesus Christ is the high priest of a perfect tabernacle. Jesus Christ's blood was perfect.

When Mary got pregnant with this high priest, the Lord sent the Holy Spirit and deposited a seed in Mary. The Lord then breathed His breath into Mary, and with His breath came His blood.

Adam was created from the dust. The Bible states that the life of the flesh is in the blood. When God breathed into Adam, blood flowed along with the breath of God. Adam also inherited God's blood. Since Adam came from the dust, and because he sinned, the dust which was **"flesh"** contaminated God's blood. Therefore, God decided to send His blood through the Word.

The Word became flesh with the blood of God. Nothing other than the blood of Jesus wrapped up in the word of God can wash away our sins. When we realize how much power there is in the blood, we will not be afraid. The priest can only take in the blood one at a time, but the blood of Jesus gives everyone access at the same time.

Whenever the Israelites had to fight a battle they would sacrifice an animal and get a blood covering over them.

Jesus Christ entered only once having obtained eternal redemption; He did not have to die again. If blood drips for three days out of a human it will dry up. However, when Jesus Christ died and was in the grave three days, all of His blood was already drained from His body.

We know from Scriptures that Jesus was not going to see corruption. God preserved Jesus Christ in the grave for three days. Mary Magdalene came to embalm Jesus, but God had made sure that all the blood and water were drained out of Him.

All human being has eight pints of blood. We know from studies that doctors have verified that when blood and water were drained from the body it can be preserved for a longer time. What we learned from doctors' theories is a good reason why Jesus' body didn't rot.

The Bible states that Jesus Christ entered into the tabernacle of God. This tabernacle is in Heaven. Where was the blood of Jesus Christ for three days? It didn't go in the grave. Every drop of Jesus' his blood was taken into heaven. God didn't have any intentions of spilling what He needed to wash away our sins; He was not going to waste it.

When we think of Calvary, we visualize the crowd screaming at Jesus, and the soldiers scourging Him. We imagine His flesh falling like strips of ribbon on His body.

As Jesus carried the old rugged cross to the top of the hill, what we didn't see was the Holy Spirit and the angels walking around in the crowd and collecting every drop of blood falling from Jesus' veins.

Jesus blood is incorruptible; and even though it dripped to the ground it could not dry on the earth nor could the earth soak it up. Jesus' blood was not consumable. Only what is corruptible goes back to the earth. I believe that the Holy Spitir with the angels standing around collected Jesus' blood and held on to it for three days.

According to the Word of God, Jesus was in the grave for three days. He is the High Priest, and now God has sent the Holy Spirit into the tomb where Heaven's High priest laid to resurrect His body.

The High Priest in the Old Testament had to kill a lamb, but Jesus Christ is the Lamb, and He also fulfilled the role of the High Priest. John the Apostle stated that Jesus was *"the lamb of God that was slain from the foundation of the World." Revelation 13:8*

God sent the Holy Spirit into the tomb. He didn't go empty handed; He put the priestly robe on Jesus. This robe of righteousness wasn't sewn by a tailor. This robe was made by the Father Himself, and the Holy Spirit delivered it.

Mary thought Jesus was the gardener when she first saw Him near the tomb. However, He was wearing His Heavenly Priestly Garment. Jesus Christ fulfilled the priestly office. This priestly robe had all our names written on it.

I believe Jesus recieved His blood from the Holy Spirit while the angels stood around and carried it into Heaven.

The story of the lepers being cleansed and the bird flying into the sky, is symbolic of Jesus Christ's resurrection when He took His own blood into heaven. There were times, after Jesus Christ was resurrected, that He demonstrated how resurrected bodies would function.

When He walked through the walls, He was supernatural flesh. When He ate with His disciples, He demonstrated that supernatural flesh also eats. At the marriage supper of the Lamb our supernatural bodies will eat.

Jesus took His blood and sprinkled the Ark of God in Heaven that was in the tabernacle. The throne that was the Judgment Seat of God became the Mercy Seat of God. Jesus cleansed the tabernacle completely with His blood.

In the book of Revelation John asked who was worthy to open the seals; nobody was found worthy in the Kingdom of heaven. Nobody was worthy enough to open the seals that contained the great wrath that would be poured out on the earth. Jesus Christ is the only person worthy to open the seals.

We will lay down our crown at the feet of Jesus Christ, because we couldn't get a crown unless we accepted the redemptive work of Jesus Christ.

When saints get to Heaven all pain and earthly marks disappears. However, the marks on Jesus body remains for ever. Jesus Christ is the only person who still bears the nail scars and marks all over his body. Zechariah said when Jesus Christ appears the Jews will look on him whom they have pierced. The marks will still be visible. He would have been in Heaven for over 2,000 years before returning to see about the Jews, yet the scars will be just as fresh on his body as the day he was crucified.

Throughout the world various religions have been established. Some say Krishna died, and Mohammed died; however, when we get to Heaven there will be no dispute that Jesus died for our sins. Only one person will have a mark; that's why Jesus is keeping the marks on his body so there will be no dispute over his death.

Elijah, Enoch, the disciples, and even the prophets who were crucified upside down will have their body restored. Only one person will be recognized for being slain for us.

The tabernacle of God is where our works done on earth will be tried. The white throne judgment is where we will meet with God to be judged. If our works didn't give God glory, our works will be burned.

I heard a story of a person who had a vision of the white throne judgment. During the judgment, a preacher stood before God with several books filled with his works. When his works was put in the fire they burned up because he never glorified God. The preacher entered the rest of God, but he received no crown.

Another old lady stood before God with only one book filled with her works. All she ever did was offer up prayers for Pastors and their families. When her works was put in the fire it melted, fell to the ground and became gold. Jesus picked up the gold and made a crown for the lady because of her faithfulness; she became a ruler over many and entered into the rest of God.

Every morning we wake up, we need to apply the blood of Jesus to our lives. We don't need to kill a lamb anymore; the blood of Jesus is available even now. He entered into the tabernacle once and for all. Every time we make a mistake, He points to His blood which is sprinkled on the mercy seat, and is as fresh as the day He was crucified. Jesus tells the Father to forgive us because He has purchased us with His blood.

The blood gives us access to many things; I would like to mention three very important ones:-

1. The opportunity to call God... "Our Father" (Our Salvation).

2. We have the right to enter into His presence covered with the blood, using the name Of Jesus.

3. The Oil (the Anointing) always comes after the blood. This causes the Holy Spirit to help us get an audience with the Father instantly.

When we apply the blood to our lives, our prayer life will change drastically, and we will grow in God. Thank God for **"THE BLOOD."**

# CHAPTER SEVENTEEN

# RECONNECTING THE PRIEST LINE

In Exodus 19, forty-six days after the children of Israel left Egypt, Moses went up to Mount Sinai to meet with God. The Lord told Moses that He had a plan for Israel.

> *"And Moses went up unto God, and the Lord called unto him out of the mountain, saying, thus shalt thou say to the house of Jacob, and tell the children of Israel; Ye have seen what I did unto the Egyptians, and how I bare you on eagles' wings, and bought you unto Myself. Now therefore, if ye will obey My voice indeed, and keep My covenant, then ye shall be a peculiar treasure unto Me above all people: for all the earth is mine: And ye shall be unto Me a kingdom of priests, and an holy nation. These are the words which thou shalt speak unto the children of Israel."*
> *(Exodus 19:3-6)*

We know that God cannot lie and He cannot change. Also, whenever He speaks a word it always comes to pass.

In Exodus 12, God told Moses that He was changing the calendar of the children of Israel. He told Moses that this month would be the beginning of months to them. This was the month Nissan Abib on the Jewish calendar, and March/April on the English calendar.

It was the beginning of Israel's year. God said that on the tenth day of the month the entire nation of Israel was to take a lamb and keep it for four days. The lamb was to be without blemish and was to be killed on the fourteenth day at 3 o'clock, which was the evening sacrifice. The lamb was killed at three o'clock in the afternoon; the same time that Jesus died on the cross.

The lamb had to be eaten during that night. They were to take the blood of the lamb and sprinkle the two upper door posts of the house where they were going to eat the lamb.

This story is well known by most Bible reading Christians. Over the years, we have overlooked some very important features. We believe there were three million Jewish men, besides women and children. Therefore, we believe that some six million plus persons left Egypt. After all, there was a mixed congregation. This means that there were some Egyptians that got under the blood. The promise was not when I see the Israelites, but when I see the blood, I will pass over you.

One of the most fascinating revelations in this story is the perfect time of preparation by God. I believe a minimum of three million lambs had to be prepared and used for every Israelite house in Egypt; and each one had to be a male unblemished lamb. If these lambs were not unblemished their blood would not represent the blood of Jesus.

This is just amazing considering that all had to be male, which portrays Jesus. All had to be unblemished (Christ without sin). All had to be kept for four days symbolizing four thousand years of religion (shadows or types) before Christ was crucified.

It is also amazing if you think about it in the natural. However, there is nothing natural about it. God told Abraham that his seed would be a stranger in a strange land and that they would be afflicted for four hundred years. The entire dispensation of promise was four hundred and thirty years.

This is the reason why when Jesus went to raise Lazarus from the dead, it was said that he was buried four days already and by now he stinketh.

Throughout the Old Testament, God referred to religious ceremonies that gave off a foul odor: as a stench in His nostril. This is what four thousand years of rituals did. If a sacrifice was not from the heart, God did not receive it.

In the Book of Exodus, Chapter Nineteen, on the fifteenth day of Nissan Abib or the month March/April, the children of Israel left Egypt. It was from this day that forty-six days were counted, being the day God called Moses up to Mount Sinai. God told Moses to have the people sanctify themselves for three days, and then He was going to come down and make them a Kingdom of Priests.

It is obvious that the children of Israel went through the rituals of sanctification, but they were not changed. Moses knew this, and told God the people could not come up to Mount Sinai. God told Moses to let the people move away and just he and Aaron were to come up to Mount Sinai. God was about to demonstrate the feast of Pentecost.

Have you noticed that Moses went up to Mount Sinai on the forty-sixth day? The people sanctified themselves for three days, and on the fiftieth day after they left Egypt, God descended on the top of Mount Sinai.

The Aaronic priest line was a temporary priest line that God asked Moses to establish. God established an eternal priest line long before Moses was born. Since the separation of Abraham and Lot because of strife between their herdsmen, Lot was taken captive. Abraham took his three hundred and eighteen trained servants and went and rescued Lot.

*"And he brought back all the goods, and also brought again his brother Lot, and his goods, and the women also, and the people." (Genesis 14:16)*

While this was going on, Abraham met Melchizedek King of Salem, the priest of the Most High God. Abraham paid tithes to this priest line and the King/Priest had communion with him. This Melchizedek's priest line is the eternal priest line that Jesus came through.

*"And Melchizedek King of Salem* (name of ancient *Jerusalem) brought forth bread and wine: and he was the*

*priest of the most high God. And he blessed him, and said, blessed be Abram of the most high God, possessor of heaven and earth: and blessed be the most high God, which hath delivered thine enemies into thy hand. And he gave him tithes of all." (Genesis 14:18-20)*

*"In Judah is God known: his name is great in Israel.*

*In Salem also is his tabernacle, and his dwelling place in Zion." (Psalms 76:1-2)*

*"The Lord hath sworn, and will not repent, thou art a priest forever after the order of Melchizedek." (Psalm 110:4)*

*"For every High Priest taken from among men is ordained for men in things pertaining to God, that he may offer both gifts and sacrifices for sins: And no man taketh this honor unto himself, but he that is called of God, as was Aaron. So also Christ glorified not himself to be made an High Priest; but He that said unto Him, Thou art my Son today have I begotten thee. As He saith also in another place, thou art a priest forever after the order of Melchizedek." (Hebrews 5:1, 4-6)*

As we continue to read this passage of scripture, it shows how Jesus offered prayers and supplications with strong crying and tears unto Him that was able to save Him from death. Hebrews 5:10 called Jesus a High Priest after the order of Melchizedek.

*"Which hope we have as an anchor of the soul, both sure and steadfast, and which entereth into that within the veil; whether the forerunner is for us entered, even Jesus, made an high priest forever after the order of Melchizedek" (Hebrews 6:19-20)*

Here is a list of some facts about Melchizedek.
1) King of Salem, ancient Jerusalem. (Hebrews 7:1; Genesis 14:18)
2) Priest of God in Abraham's day. (Hebrews 7:1; Genesis 14:18)

3) Met Abraham returning from his military victory. (Hebrews 7:2; Genesis 14:16-18)

4) Abraham gave him a tenth of the spoils. (Hebrews 7:2; Genesis 14:16-24)

5) Was called King of Righteousness. (Hebrews 7:2)

6) Called King of Salem, or King of Peace. (Hebrews 7:2; Genesis 4:18)

7) Had no descendants: without recorded father or motherand without recorded beginning of days or end of life. (Hebrews 7:3, 6)

   He had a father, mother, birth and death, but these were not recorded, so that he could be a type of Christ, who was an eternal being really without beginning and ending. (Micah 5:2; Isaiah 9:6-7; John 1:1-2; Hebrews 6:1-8)

8) Made a type of Christ so that Christ could be made a priest after His order. (Hebrews 5:6, 10; 6:15-20; 7:1-10, 15-21)

9) He was an ordinary man. (Hebrews 7:4)

10) He was greater than Abraham.

It was customary among ancient nations to give a tenth of the spoils of war to the object of their worship. When God chose a temporary priest line, He chose to come through one of Jacob sons, Levi. This is where we get the Levitical priest line headed by Aaron and his sons. Levi was one of Jacob's sons and his tribe inherited the temporary priest line.

Jesus came through the tribe of Judah. This tribe did not have priests. Jacob prophesied that this King was coming through Judah. Jesus came through Judah and is King, Priest, and Lamb.

David, who was the first King of Judah, was the closest person in the tribe of Judah to being King and Priest. He ate the priest bread, and danced in a priest ephod.

This is interesting because Jesus came through the tribe of Judah, and was both Priest and King. No one could become a high priest unless they were baptized by another high priest. This is the reason why Jesus was baptized by John the Baptist.

No one saw John as a High Priest, but if one were to look closely they will discover and conclude that John the Baptist was indeed a high priest. Both of John's parents came through priest lines.

*"There was in the days of Herod, the King of Judea, a certain priest named Zacharias, of the course of Abia: and his wife was of the daughters of Aaron, and her name was Elizabeth." (Luke 1:5)*

John should have naturally inherited the priest line, but there was only one priest in the Melchizedek line. John the Baptist came to prepare the way of the Lord.

The angel told Zacharias, John's father, that the child's name shall be called John. They objected saying none of his kindred was of that name. John was not going to be in the Priest Line of his kindred, he was only concerned with connecting the Melchizedek Priest Line.

When Mary was pregnant with Jesus, she went to salute Elizabeth. The Bible declares that the baby (John) leaped in Elizabeth's womb for joy. From our studies, we are told that for six months John was like a dead fetus in his mother's womb. He did not move until Mary came and saluted his mother.

This happened because the Holy Spirit was bearing witness of Jesus as the Messiah, the Christ, and the Savior of the world. Only the Holy Spirit could have done this. When John was talking about Jesus before he saw and baptized Him, he said that he did not know Him, but He (The Father) who sent him said the one whom he baptized and saw the Spirit descending like a dove and resting upon and remaining on Him, is the one who will have the Spirit without measure.

This is interesting because the Lord took of the anointing that He gave to Moses and anointed the seventy elders. This is called the Mosaic Portion. There was an Elijah's portion of which Elisha received a double portion.

In the thirteenth Chapter of 2 Kings, when Elisha was sick and about to die, King Joash tried to get a triple portion from Elisha. God has given Jesus the anointing without measure. (Hallelujah!)

John continued to tell the people that he was not the Messiah, but only a voice of one crying in the wilderness preparing the way of the Lord. He told them that there was one who was coming after him whose shoes he was not worthy to unloose; and that He would baptize with the Holy Ghost and with fire.

When Jesus came to John to be baptized, John said he needed to be baptized by Him. Jesus responded suffer it to be so now, so fulfill all righteousness. What Jesus was saying was if He was not baptized by another High Priest, He could not fulfill the law of God and could not rightfully take His place in the priest line.

If you notice, He did not go to Caiaphas or any of the other high priests from the Levitical line. John did not take his father's job of being a high priest, but he came to reconnect the priest line. When John baptized Jesus, he reconnected the eternal priest line which only had one high priest in the Melchizedek order, and that one High Priest is Jesus Christ...praise God!

# CHAPTER EIGHTEEN

# ROYAL PRIEST LINE

*"For as the rain cometh down, and the snow from heaven, and returneth not thither, but watereth the earth, and maketh it bring forth and bud, that it may give seed to the sower, and bread to the eater: So shall my word be that goeth forth out of my mouth: it shall not return unto me void, but it shall accomplish that which I please, and it shall prosper in the thing whereto I sent it." (Isaiah 55:10-11)*

*"God is not a man, that He should lie; neither the son of man, that He should repent: hath He said, and shall He not do it? Or hath He spoken, and shall He not make it good?" (Numbers 23:19)*

God told Jeremiah in the first chapter of his book, verse twelve, that He will hasten to perform His word. In **Psalm 138:2**, we are told that God magnifies His word above His name.

Let us now consider a few Scripture references to show that the study of the blood of Jesus confirmed His word, as well as, introduced us to a Royal Priest Line.

In **Exodus 19**, you will recall God spoke a word just before He introduced the children of Israel to the first day of Pentecost or (the feast of Pentecost.) He said that He wanted a '**Kingdom of Priests.**' The word **'kingdom'** speaks of a **king** over a **domain.** It also speaks of **royalty.** Now we can see clearly why the Leviticus priest line was a temporary line. From Aaron to Caiaphas the high priest there was no one that could claim royalty.

It was after Jesus was crucified, ascended to heaven, and sent the promise of the Holy Ghost fifty days after He was resurrected, did God allow Peter, in I Peter, to call us a royal priest hood.

*"But ye are a chosen generation, a royal priesthood, an holy nation, a peculiar people; that ye should shew forth the praises of him who hath called you out of darkness into his marvelous light." (I Peter 2:9)*

If you would take another look at **Exodus 19:5-6**, you would have to conclude that God keeps His word. However, His word became reality when the Royal King from the only Royal Priest Line shed His blood.

*"Now therefore, if ye will obey my voice indeed, and keep my covenant, then ye shall be a peculiar treasure unto me above all people: for all the earth is mine: and ye shall be unto me a kingdom of priests, and an holy nation. These are the words which thou shalt speak unto the children of Israel." (Exodus 19:5-6)*

We have so much to thank God for when it comes to the blood of Jesus. We all have heard and believe that He was wounded for our transgression, He was bruised for our iniquities, the chastisement of our peace was upon Him; and with His stripes we are healed.

If we hear a thing often, at first we may say it is just another statement, but if we allow the reality of what happened to sink in and take root then we are able to appreciate it.

In **Hebrews 9**, we can come boldly because of the blood. The priest in the Old Testament did not have this privilege. They had to take blood in with them and sprinkle the furniture in the Tabernacle. Our High Priest was both The Priest and the Lamb, and He sprinkled all the furniture of the tabernacle, now all we have to do is be washed in the blood, then we can come in boldly.

In **Ezekiel Chapter 28,** I pointed out to you a description of lucifer's robe or covering which was similar to that of the high priest of the Levitical order.

However, the High Priest of the Levitical order had robes with twelve precious stones representing the twelve tribes of Israel. This was made after the pattern of a High Priest's robe in heaven. Remember it was God's plan to have a kingdom of priests. The kingdom is the pronouncement of a king. It is very clear that a king had to die. Royalty only comes through a king. When Jesus died, He made it possible for us to have a royal priest line. That's the reason we are a royal priest hood, a peculiar people. Only royal blood can make us royalty. Praise God for Jesus!

# CHAPTER NINETEEN

# THE ROYAL LINE
# OF CHRIST VISION

In 1993, God spoke to me about people in the world with similar experiences as the characters listed in the blood line of Christ.

There are those who have been raped, or molested by family members and older people. Also, there are persons who have willingly committed adultery and prostitution: both male and female. Society has counted most of these people out, and in most cases the victims have counted themselves out.

Many church folks who have experienced one or more of these life styles have been set free, but now pretend as if they have never sinned. They now talk about these people who can't find their way out.

God has given me a vision to go in search of these people, and let them know that He has made provision for them in the blood line of Jesus Christ.

In 1997, the very first national crusade/conference called '**In Search of the Royal Line of Christ**' was held in Freeport, Grand Bahama, at the Camelot Room, Bahamas Princess Hotel.

In 1998, the first international crusade/conference was held in the United States at the Georgia World Congress Centre, Atlanta, Georgia.

To date, we have held over twenty-three crusades/conferences. It is my sincere hope that one day the entire world will see and become a part of the passion that is burning in me. I strongly believe that when Jesus commissioned His disciples and told them to go into all the world, He had these people in mind. These people would be considered as the stones which the builders rejected.

As was stated in an earlier chapter, I believe God has given this world a prophetic week. Each day of the week is as a thousand years. Each day God has done a new thing. From Adam to Noah is a thousand years or the first day. From Noah to Abraham is a thousand years or the second day. From Abraham to David is a thousand years or the third day. From King David to King Jesus is a thousand years or the fourth day of man's prophetic week.

Jesus left earth two thousand years ago, which completes the sixth day of man's week. This is the day that God made man and told him to take dominion.

I believe that according to our English calendar, we are in the seventh day or the seventh millennium. God has always done something different each day in man's week. I am persuaded that He is doing likewise in this day. I am convinced that He has made a people for this day, and these people are the stones which the builders rejected. These people are the rejects of society: drug addicts, prostitutes, incest, rapists and their victims, alcoholics, and others of like status.

This last day God will make them the head and not the tail. He will make them the head of the corner just like He has done with Jesus.

> *"The stone which the builders refused is become the head stone of the corner.*
> *This is the LORD's doing; it is marvelous in our eyes. This is the day which the LORD hath made; we will rejoice and be glad in it. Save now, I beseech thee, O LORD: O LORD, I beseech thee, send now prosperity." (Psalm 118:22-25)*

God makes a people for a day, and I believe that God is making a perfect people for today, His day. He said that what He is doing is marvelous in our eyes. He also talked about a people who were poor and promised to send them in that same day prosperity. This is where my heart is; and this is why I do two conferences a year.

*"To whom coming, as unto a living stone, disallowed indeed of men, but chosen of God, and precious, ye also, as lively stones, are built up a spiritual house, an holy priesthood, to offer up spiritual sacrifices, acceptable to God by Jesus Christ.*

*Wherefore also it is contained in the scripture, Behold, I lay in Sion a chief corner stone, elect, precious: and he that believeth on him shall not be confounded.*

*Unto you therefore which believe he is precious: but unto them which be disobedient, the stone which the builders disallowed, the same is made the head of the corner, and a stone of stumbling, and a rock of offense, even to them which stumble at the word, being disobedient: whereunto also they were appointed.*

*But ye are a chosen generation, a royal priesthood, an holy nation, a peculiar people; that ye should shew forth the praises of him who hath called you out of darkness into his marvelous light: which in time past were not a people, but are now the people of God: which had not obtained mercy, but now have obtained mercy." (1 Peter 2:4-10)*

I believe the reason why the Holy Spirit spoke through the apostle Peter saying, this people will show forth the praises of God is because many times people who grew up in church thinking they always had a good life, seemed not to be excited about their God.

However, the people whom God delivered from pits and holes have accepted that He had done something for them. These people always praise God with a passion that far exceeds the norm. They are not ashamed to show it or for it to be heard. These people, most of the time, are very loud with their praise.

I believe this day is made for Royal Line members. These people have no one else to praise or worship for bringing them out. They know that if it had not been for God they would not have come out. Praise God! Hallelujah!

# CHAPTER TWENTY

# IN SEARCH OF THE ROYAL LINE OF CHRIST

As was stated in the previous chapter, I carried a vision for four years on the inside of me. It was not until the fall of 1997 that this vision became a reality.

In this Chapter, I will discuss the characteristics of people I have examined in God's word. These people backgrounds have inspired me to go in search of persons who are having similar experiences and introduce them to the blood of Jesus Christ. As a result of this, the Royal Line of Christ Conference was initiated.

*"The book of the generation of Jesus Christ, the son of David, the son of Abraham. Abraham begat Isaac; and Isaac begat Jacob; and Jacob begat Judas and his brethren; and Judas begat Phares and Zara of Thamar; and Phares begat Esrom; and Esrom begat Aram; and Aram begat Aminadab; and Aminadab begat Naasson; and Naasson begat Salmon; and Salmon begat Booz of Rachab; and Booz begat Obed of Ruth; and Obed begat Jesse; and Jesse begat David the King; and David the King begat Solomon of her that had been the wife of Urias (Bathsheba.)"*
*(Matthew 1:1-6)*

These Scriptures list some of the persons that are in the genealogy of Jesus Christ. The Lord allowed me to look closely at the life of some of them. God has ministered to my heart that they are in the genealogy because of the blood of Jesus Christ.

# Judah

From the prophecy of Jacob in **Genesis 49,** we know that Jesus was scheduled to come through the tribe of Judah. In **Genesis 38**, Judah's oldest son Er, married Tamar.

The Bible says that Er was wicked in the sight of the Lord, and the Lord slew him. After Er died, Judah gave his second son Onan, to be husband to Tamar and raise up seed to his brother.

When Onan went in unto Tamar and realized the seed would not be his, he spilled the seed on the ground. This displeased God and he slew him also.

Judah had a third son named Shelah. He promised Tamar that if she would remain a widow, Shelah would become her husband and she could have children by him. Judah feared the death of his third son and did not give Shelah to Tamar as he promised.

One day as Judah was going to Timnath to shear his sheep; Tamar took off her widow's attire, covered herself with a veil and sat in the open. Judah saw her and thinking she was a harlot, requested that he go in unto her. Tamar asked him what he would give her. Judah promised to send her a kid, and gave her his signet, bracelet and staff as a pledge.

As soon as this was done Tamar left; she took off the veil and put on her widow's garment.

Judah sent the kid he had promised Tamar with a servant, but the servant could not find her. He told Judah that no one knew of her, and was unable to help him because no harlot was in the way to Timnath.

Three months later Judah was told that his daughter-in-law, Tamar, had played the harlot and was with child. Judah asked that Tamar be fetched and burned.

When Tamar was brought before her father-in-law, she told him that she was pregnant for the person who had left his signet, bracelet and staff with her. Judah knew the signet with his seal, name or emblem, and which was worn around his neck belonged to him.

Signets which were indispensible with men of wealth or position were used for the certification of legal documents. The one having it can use it for forgery of a person's character and credit. Bracelets were worn by men of wealth and position. Sometimes the signet was a part of the bracelet.

The staff had the owner's name on it, and the names of the owner's ancestors to show their lineage or inheritance. These items were the most important pieces of legislation that a man could have for business. They were held by important wealthy men of the East and Judah had all three; now they were in the possession of a woman he wants to have burned.

Judah did not know that the woman whom he had slept with was his daughter-in-law, Tamar. Judah repented, and Tamar's life was spared. It was discovered that Tamar was pregnant with twins. She had the twins and called them Pharez and Zara.

In the book of Matthew the first chapter Judah, Tamar, and Pharez are listed in the blood line or genealogy of Jesus. May I remind you that once God gave his word, He cannot lie, and the word cannot return to him void. In **Genesis**, He had already spoken through Jacob that Shiloh (Jesus) was coming through Judah.

*"A bastard shall not enter into the congregation of the Lord; even to his tenth generation shall he not enter into the congregation of the Lord." (Deuteronomy 23:2)*

This means that because of incest bastard children were born, and no one from the tribe of Judah could enter into or become the leader of the people or congregation, until the tenth generation. It was the Prophet Isaiah who through the Holy Spirit prophesied that Jesus was coming through the lineage of David, and was going to be established upon the throne of David.

*"For unto us a Child is born, unto us a Son is given: and the government shall be upon His shoulder: and His name shall be called Wonderful, Counsellor, The mighty God, The*

*everlasting Father, The Prince of peace. Of the increase of His government and peace there shall be no end, upon the throne of David, and upon his kingdom, to order it, and to establish it with judgment and with justice from henceforth even for ever. The zeal of the LORD of hosts will perform this." (Isaiah 9:6-7)*

## THE TENTH GENERATION FROM JUDAH

*"Now these are the generation of Perez: Perez begat Hezron, and Hezron begat Ram, and Ram begat Amminadab, and Amminadab begat Nahshon, and Nahshon begat Salmon, and Salmon begat Boaz, and Boaz begat Obed, and Obed begat Jesse, and Jesse begat David." (Ruth 4:18-22)*

Jesus came through the tribe of Judah.

Sometimes when we receive a word from the Lord it seems as if it will never come to pass. I study the Bible, I discovered that God cannot lie. His word has never returned to him void. He is always watching over His word, and He will hasten to perform it.

This is something that satan himself knows, but will never admit. Be assured that one day he will. satan has never heard God said anything that did not come to pass; no matter how long and hard he fought its manifestation, even if it is down to the person's tenth generation.

God saw Jesus in Abraham's bosom forty-two generations down.

As we have seen in the story of Judah and Tamar, David represents the fulfillment of the tenth generation from Judah coming through the lineage of one of Judah's twin sons, Pharez.

Throughout the tenth generation as recorded in Ruth 4:18-22, there are no ladies listed in the genealogy or blood line of Jesus Christ, but in **Matthew 1:5** they are recorded. These ladies are Tamar, Rahab, Ruth and Bethsheba.

# RAHAB CONNECTON

The story of Tamar depicts a desperate woman, who took drastic measures. She committed incest to have an inheritance in the Judah line, which is the King's line. Tamar disguised herself as a prostitute or harlot, but Rahab was a harlot.

*"And Joshua the son of Nun sent out of Shittim two men to spy secretly, saying, go view the land, even Jericho, and they went, and came into a harlot's house, named Rahab, and lodged there." (Joshua 2:1)*

Rahab was in the genealogy of Jesus because of faith and works. She knew that God was giving Jericho to Israel and she wanted to have her family and her life spared.

The King of Jericho sent out his men to Rahab's house and requested that she released the men who came to her. She told them that the men came, but she did not know where they were because by the time the city gate was shut the men had left.

Her suggestion to the king's men was to chase after the two men and they were sure to overtake them. This sounded reasonable and quite an easy task for the king's men. The Jordan had overflowed its banks and it would have been impossible, in the natural, for the spies to have gotten far. Rahab made the suggestion knowing that she had hidden the two men on the roof of her house.

*"But she had brought them up to the roof of the house, and hid them with the stalks of flax, which she had laid in order upon the roof." (Joshua 2:6)*

This woman did her works; now listen to her faith.

*"For we have heard how the Lord dried up the water of the Red Sea for you, when ye came out of Egypt; and what ye did unto the two kings of the Amorites, that were on the other side of Jordan. Sihon and Og, whom ye utterly destroyed." (Joshua 2:10)*

*"So then faith cometh by hearing, and hearing by the word of God." (Romans 10:17)*

This woman chose to have faith in the God of the children of Israel.

*"And as soon as we had heard these things, our hearts did melt, neither did there remain any more courage in any man, because of you: for the LORD your God, he is God in heaven above, and in earth beneath." (Joshua 2:11)*

While Rahab confessed the fear of herself and her people, she did her work and made her request known. As a reward for hiding the spies, she requested that no harm come to her and her household.

*"Now therefore, I pray you, swear unto me by the LORD, since I have shewed you kindness, that ye will also show kindness unto my father's house, and give me a true token: and that ye will save alive my father, and my mother, and my brethren, and my sisters, and all that they have, and deliver our lives from death." (Joshua 2:12-13)*

The two spies agreed to the request made by Rahab, and then she let them down by a scarlet cord through a window. The spies instructed Rahab that the same scarlet cord she used to let them down be hung in the window. By doing this, she and her family members would be saved. No one was allowed to leave the house. The promise was only for those who abide in the house.

When we remind ourselves of the building of the tabernacle and the materials used, we know that one of the colors was scarlet according to **Exodus 25:4.** The four linens that stood at the gate of the Tabernacle were a shadow of the four gospels that speak of the earthly ministry of Jesus. Scarlet speaks of the suffering Savior. The scarlet cord typifies the blood of Jesus.

The lives of the spies were saved by the blood of Jesus. Rahab used the scarlet cord to mark her house, and Joshua sent the two spies in to bring out her family. This house was rescued by the blood of Jesus. It was the blood of Jesus that kept one house standing in an entire city that fell down. Even though the scarlet cord was symbolic of the blood of Jesus, when Rahab and her family came to the nation of Israel they had to be left outside the camp of Israel.

> *"And the young men that were spies went in, and brought out Rahab, and her father, and her mother, and her brethren, and all that she had; and they brought out all her kindred, and left them without the camp of Israel."* *(Joshua 6:23)*

The camp of Israel symbolizes heaven as was the case of the ceremony of the cleansing of the leper. In cleansing of the leper, the priest had to leave the camp of Israel go outside to where the leper was, and sprinkle him with blood before the leper was allowed to enter the camp of Israel.

The same procedure applied to Rahab and her family. They were left outside the camp until all the men in her family were circumcised. This shows us that no matter how good we think we are or how much good that we have done, no one is going to be able to enter into heaven without the blood of Christ. We must not forget that leprosy is a symbol of sin and had to be cleansed with the blood of Jesus. Rahab and her family were Gentiles in sin and had to go through the same process as lepers.

> *"And the leper in whom the plague is, his clothes shall be rent, and his head bare, and he shall put a covering upon his upper lip, and shall cry, unclean, unclean. All the days wherein the plague shall be in him he shall be defiled; he is unclean: he shall dwell alone; without the camp shall his habitation be." (Leviticus 13:45-46)*

After the circumcision of the males in Rahab's family, she and her family were allowed into the camp. Rahab married a prominent man of Israel named Salmon, and they had a son named Boaz. Boaz married Ruth.

# RUTH CONNECTION

To fully appreciate the Ruth connection in the genealogy or lineage or blood line of Jesus, we must examine her journey. Most Bible believing Christians think that Ruth's story starts with her mother-in-law, Naomi. Naomi's story is just one phase that culminated in the perfect will of God. Let us see where Ruth began.

# RUTH'S ORIGIN

*"And Elimelech Naomi's husband died; and she was left, and her two sons. And they took them wives of the women of Moab; the name of the one was Orpah, and the name of the other Ruth: and they dwelled there about ten years." (Ruth 1:3-4)*

Here we see that Ruth came from a nation that got started by incest.

In **Genesis 19**, God destroyed the city of Sodom and Gomorrah. The angel of God saw to it that Lot and his family escaped the destruction. As they were leaving the city, Lot's wife looked back and she became a pillar of salt. Lot and his two daughters escaped to Zoar. They settled in the mountains and lived in a cave.

Lot was old, and there was no other man to lie with the daughters so they made a decision to get their father to drink wine. Afterwards, they would lie with him and have children in order to preserve the family line. As a result of Lot being drunk and not knowing what had taken place, both daughters conceived and had sons by their father.

*"And it came to pass on the morrow, that the firstborn said unto the younger, behold, I lay yesternight with my father: let us make him drink wine this night also; and go thou in, and lie with him, that we may preserve seed of our father. And they made their father drink wine that night also: and the younger arose, and lay with him; and he perceived not when she lay down, nor when she arose. Thus were both*

*the daughters of Lot with child by their father. And the first-born bare a son, and called his name Moab: the same is the father of the Moabites unto this day. And the younger, she also bare a son, and called his name Benammi: the same is the father of the children of Ammon unto this day."*
*(Genesis 19:34-38)*

The Moabites and the Ammonites were thorns in Israel's life throughout their wilderness experience, yet Ruth came from the Moabites. This nation did not know the God of Abraham, Isaac and Jacob. The people of this tribe were idolaters: yet Elimelech, Naomi's husband, moved his family from Bethlehem-Judah (the house of bread and praise) to the land of Moab.

Elimelech died and his two sons Mahlon and Chilon married Orpah and Ruth, women of Moab. Mahlon and Chilon also died. Naomi was left with her two daughters-in-law. Naomi felt she had lost everything and that God was against her. She gave her two daughters-in-law the option to return to their families as she was returning to her native home in Bethlehem-Judah.

Orpah accepted the offer and returned to her native land and back to idol practices, but Ruth declined. Ruth had a change of heart, and after being introduced to Naomi's God fell in love with the only true God. This attachment to the only true God got her in the blood line of Jesus Christ.

*"And Ruth said, intreat me not to leave thee, or to return from following after thee: for whither thou goest, I will go; and where thou lodgest, I will lodge: thy people shall be my people, and thy God my God: where thou diest, will I die, and there will I be buried: the Lord do so to me, and more also, if ought but death part thee and me." (Ruth 1:16-17)*

Ruth became the possession of her mother-in-law. Naomi had a kinsman named Boaz. Boaz was a wealthy man and a direct descendant of Elimelech, Naomi's husband.

*"And Naomi had a kinsman of her husband's, a mighty man of wealth, of the family of Elimelech; and his name was Boaz." (Ruth 2:1)*

Ruth after gleaning in Boaz's field, capturing his attention, and him paying the kinsman dowry to Naomi, became his wife. They had a son and called him Obed.

Obed had a son named Jesse. Jesse had a son named David. Jesus came through the direct lineage of David.

Ruth is now in the blood line of Jesus, and even though her ancestors were involved in incestuous relationships incest was not for Ruth. She found the perfect will for her life, which was hidden in God before the foundation of the world.

*"And Salmon begat Boaz, and Boaz begat Obed, and Obed begat Jesse, and Jesse begat David." (Ruth 4:21-22)*

# BETHSHEBA'S CONNECTION

At the time when kings went out to war, David decided to stay at home in Jerusalem. He sent Joab, his other servants, and all of Israel to fight against Ammon.

One evening David arose from his bed and walked upon the roof of his house. He saw a woman washing herself. Bethsheba, wife of Uriah the Hittite, was a very beautiful woman.

Several questions are raised as to why this beautiful woman was washing herself in public view of the king's palace. Did she not know that such an open and close view would be a source of temptation to King David? Could there have been some desire on her part? Whatever the case, King David enquired about her and sent for her. Bethsheba came and he slept with her. Afterwards she returned to her house.

The Scripture does not insinuate any refusal or resistance on Bethsheba's part. Bethsheba became pregnant and she sent and told King David.

If you know anything about this story, you will recall how King David sent for Uriah, Bethsheba's husband inviting him to his palace. King David enquired about the war and the people. He then sent Uriah home to relax from the battle. He also sent fresh food along for him.

Uriah slept at the King's door with all of the servants. He was too loyal to the king to go home and have a good time, while the Ark of the Covenant and the children of Israel were in battle. David made Uriah drink wine until he was drunk then tried again to get him to go home, but Uriah refused. Instead, he slept in the bed at the palace with the servants of David.

David tried to hide his sin. He thought at this early stage of pregnancy, if he got Uriah to sleep with his wife he would be named the baby's father. After this did not work, David gave Uriah his own fatal letter to take to Joab.

*"And it came to pass in the morning, that David wrote a letter to Joab, and sent it by the hand of Uriah. And he wrote in the letter, saying, set ye Uriah in the forefront of the hottest battle, and retire ye from him, that he may be smitten, and die." (2 Samuel 11:14-15)*

Joab did what the King commanded, and Uriah was killed. The report of the fierce battle was sent to David. Joab allowed the anointed army of God to suffer loss, just to have one man killed. When Bethsheba heard that her husband was killed, she mourned seven days for him, and then hurriedly married the man who had her husband killed. This hasty wedding was held to hide the pregnancy, but it greatly displeased the Lord.

David at this time felt that his sins were hidden because only Joab and Bethsheba knew about it. He forgot about God who sees and records everything. God sent the prophet Nathan to King David.

The prophet Nathan told King David a story of a rich man who abused the property of a poor man. David spoke total condemnation on the man to the point where he sentenced him to death. The prophet Nathan told David that he was the man in the story. Even though David repented, he was told that the child would not live.

We can not say how old the child was, but the Lord allowed the child to be sick. David lay on his face in the dirt praying and fasting seven days and seven nights for the life of the child, yet the child died.

*"And it came to pass on the seventh day, that the child died. And the servants of David feared to tell him that the child was dead: for they said, behold, while the child was yet alive, we spake unto him, and he would not hearken unto our voice: how will he then vex himself, if we tell him that the child is dead? But when David saw that his servants whispered, David perceived that the child was dead: therefore David said unto his servants, is the child dead? And they said he is dead." (2 Samuel 12:18-19)*

King David got up, washed and anointed himself, changed his clothes, went into the house of the Lord and worshipped God. From here, he went to his own house where they set bread before him and he ate. David comforted his wife Bethsheba, went in unto her and she conceived. She had a son and they called him Solomon. Solomon succeeded his father David, and he became the wisest king that ever lived.

It is amazing how in today's society people past get in the way of their future. Bethsheba committed adultery, but she is still listed in the lineage of Jesus Christ.

I believe God allowed people such as Judah, Tamar, Pharez, Rahab, Ruth, Bethsheba, and many more from Abraham to Jesus: some forty-two generations; people of various backgrounds who have committed sins, to realize that He has not condemned them and still has a plan for their life.

This is what the Royal Line Of Christ Crusade/Conference is in search of; people with similar backgrounds.

# CHAPTER TWENTY-ONE

# THE BLOOD OF JESUS
# IN HEALING

We have already seen what the blood of Jesus symbolizes: the cleansing of the lepers in **Leviticus 14**. We know that leprosy is a symbol of sin, and we also know that it was sin that brought forth sickness.

*"But of the tree of the knowledge of good and evil, thou shalt not eat of it: for in the day that thou eatest thereof thou shalt surely die." (Genesis 2:17)*

This is the first promise of sickness, and it was promised because of disobedience.

The day Adam and Eve ate the fruit sickness began. Instantly, they died spiritually and began to die physically. They tried to cover themselves (nakedness/sin) by making clothes of leaves.

God in his infinite mercy showed at the very beginning that man can not produce anything that can make him whole or free him from sin. God made Adam and Eve clothes of animals' skin. This shows that only the blood of someone innocent (Jesus) will be able to cover and heal man of sin.

In the book of Genesis before God made Adam and Eve coats of skin, He promised that the Messiah would defeat the devil, the originator of sin and sickness.

*"And I will put enmity between thee and the woman, and between thy seed and her seed; it shall bruise thy head, and thou shalt bruise his heel." (Genesis 3:15)*

This is the promise of Jesus Christ defeating satan on the cross. Throughout the Bible, the people had to bring a sacrifice for sin. Before any victory in battle the people always had to apply Jesus blood. This was emphasized with the institution of the Passover before the children of Israel left Egypt. Massive healings took place; as the body of Christ, eaten on the inside, and the blood of Christ applied on the outside, protected them from death. God later reiterated the promise He made to Adam in the Garden of Eden; the benefit of a long healthy life if they walk in obedience to God's word.

*"And said, if thou wilt diligently hearken to the voice of the LORD thy God, and wilt do that which is right in His sight, and wilt give ear to His commandments, and keep all his statutes, I will put none of these diseases upon thee, which I have brought upon the Egyptians: for I am the LORD that healeth thee." (Exodus 15:26)*

## FIRST PHYSICAL HEALING
## IN ANSWER TO PRAYER

When Abraham went to Gerer, he told his wife Sarah to tell King Abimelech that she was his sister. Abraham feared that because his wife was very beautiful (fair to look upon) he would be killed. Abimelech took Sarah and he became sick. That night God visited Abimelech in a dream and told him that if he touches Sarah he was going to die.

*"But God came to Abimelech in a dream by night, and said to him, behold, thou art but a dead man, for the woman which thou hast taken; for she is a man's wife." (Genesis 20:3)*

God told Abimelech that he was the one who restricted him from touching Sarah. Abimelech were restricted not only because she was a man's wife, but also because she was the wife of one of God's prophets.

I am a believer that the prophet of God does not have to fight in the flesh for what God has given him. All he has to do is walk in obedience to God, and God will protect everything that belongs to him: his wife, his children, his possessions.

*"He suffered no man to do them wrong: yea he reproved kings for their sakes, saying, Touch not mine anointed, and do my prophets no harm." (Psalm 105:14-15)*

Abimelech called Abraham and gave him back his wife.

*"And Abimelech took sheep, and oxen, and men servants, and women servants, and gave them to Abraham, and restored him Sarah his wife.*
*And Abimelech said, Behold, my land is before thee: dwell where it pleaseth thee. And unto Sarah he said, Behold, I have given thy brother a thousand pieces of silver: behold, he is to thee a covering of the eyes, unto all that are with thee, and with all other: thus she was reproved."*
*(Genesis 20:14-16)*

Abimelech brought a blood sacrifice, as well as, a financial seed. The sheep and oxen when sacrificed represented the blood of Jesus. The money or silver was given to Abraham to purchase a veil for his wife to cover her beauty so strangers would not covet her.

*"So Abraham prayed unto God: and God healed Abimelech, and his wife, and his maidservants; and they bare children. For the LORD had fast closed up all the wombs of the house of Abimelech, because of Sarah Abraham's wife." (Genesis 20:17-18)*

This is the first recorded physical healing in answer to prayer. We can follow the Bible from Genesis to Revelation and discover many healings and miracles that have taken place, but no one put it as clearly as the prophet Isaiah.

David gave a description of the crucifixion of Jesus in **Psalm 22.** The prophet Isaiah made it clear that there was no total redemption from sin, sickness, or pain without the actual manifestation of the death of Jesus Christ.

> *"Therefore the Lord himself shall give you a sign; behold, a virgin shall conceive, and bear a son, and shall call His name Immanuel." (Isaiah 7:14)*
>
> *"For unto us a child is born, unto us a Son is given: and the government shall be upon His shoulder: and His name shall be called Wonderful, Counselor, The mighty God, The everlasting father, The Prince of Peace. Of the increase of His government and peace there shall be no end, upon the throne of David, and upon His kingdom, to order it, and to establish it with judgment and with justice from henceforth even for ever. The zeal of the LORD of hosts will perform this." (Isaiah 9:6-7)*

As was stated before, Isaiah died 700-750 years before Christ was born, but he kept on saying **'unto us' and 'our'** and he always included himself.

> *"Surely He hath borne our griefs, and carried our sorrows: yet we did esteem Him stricken, smitten of God, and afflicted. But He was wounded for our transgressions; He was bruised for our iniquities: the chastisement of our peace was upon Him; and with His stripes we are healed." (Isaiah 53:4-5)*

The writing of Isaiah has always fascinated me whenever he uses the word *'our.'* He always included himself and all of the prophets before and after him.

*"These all died in faith, not having received the promises, but having seen them afar off, and were persuaded of them, and embraced them, and confessed that they were strangers and pilgrims on the earth." (Hebrews 11:13)*

Isaiah saw the crucifixion of Jesus. He not only saw His death, but also the horrible way He was going to die. He made it very clear that because of this death, we were healed.

It is important to note that everything in God was finished from the very beginning. In the first chapter of Genesis, God said that the evening and the morning was the first, second, third, fourth, fifth, and sixth day. We have to start in the morning, but God showed us that when He starts, He is finished; so He starts in the evening.

Even though the seed of the woman was not manifested until four thousand years after the prophecy, yet Jesus is the Lamb that was slain from the foundation of the world.

*"And all that dwell upon the earth shall worship him, whose names are not written in the book of life of the Lamb slain from the foundation of the world." (Revelation 13:8)*

The prophet Isaiah and all the Old Testament prophets knew they could not get to the Father without the Son. Everyone needs a Redeemer. Isaiah made up the first fruit offering, and was only given access to the Father in Heaven after Jesus took His blood and fixed the place as stated in **St. John 14: 2- 4.**

Throughout the Old Testament, when people needed healing they would always bring a blood sacrifice. However, when Jesus walked the earth, He did not require a blood sacrifice. He was the blood sacrifice. Shortly after coming out of the wilderness after being there for forty days tempted by the devil, Jesus went by the Sea of Galilee and started hand picking some of His disciples. Afterwards, He went throughout Galilee teaching and preaching the gospel of the kingdom, and healing all manner of sickness and diseases.

*"And Jesus went about all Galilee, teaching in their syna- gogues, and preaching the gospel of the kingdom, and*

*healing all manner of sickness and all manner of disease among the people. And his fame went throughout all Syria: and they brought unto Him all sick people that were taken with divers diseases and torments, and those which were possessed with devils, and those which were lunatic, and those that had the palsy; and he healed them." (Matthew 4:23-24)*

Throughout the four gospels which describes the earthly ministry of Jesus, we see many healings and casting out of devils. Never once did Jesus say I command you in the name of Jesus to come out! Instead, He spoke to the condition or cast out the spirit, and the devil had to obey.

In Matthew Chapter Eight, the woman with the issue of blood just touched the hem of Jesus' garment. Jarius' daughter, He just spoke the word. The centurion servant, He sent the word. The Gaderene demon, He commanded to leave. The blind, deaf and dumb spirit, He cast out in different ways. Jesus was able to do this because every weapon we need is in Him. **He is the blood, He is the word, and He had the Spirit without measure.**

As was demonstrated in Acts, Chapter Three, when Peter and John went up to the Temple to pray they met a lame man who stood begging every day. Peter's statement is still the only way that we can get a person delivered from sin, sickness or demons. It is in the Name of Jesus, the only name under heaven whereby man could be saved.

*"And he gave heed unto them, expecting to receive something of them. Then Peter said, silver and gold have I none; but such as I have give I thee:*
*In the name of Jesus Christ of Nazareth rise up and walk." (Acts 3:5-6)*

When we accept Jesus Christ as Lord, we are given the power of attorney in His name. This is a privilege that is given only to those who accept Him as Lord and Savior.

*"Now we know that God heareth not sinners: but if any man be a worshipper of God, and doeth his will, him he heareth." (St. John 9:31)*

This statement was used by the blind man who Jesus healed in St. John, Chapter Nine. We must make it very clear that God hears every sinner that is repentant and is truly seeking salvation. The sinner does not have the authority to use the name of Jesus. Not to heal the sick, the blind, cast out demons, or to speak in the authority of His word. However, immediately his sins are washed away, these privileges become his.

*"And these signs shall follow them that believe; In my name shall they cast out devils; they shall speak with new tongues; They shall take up serpents; and if they drink any deadly thing, it shall not hurt them; they shall lay hands on the sick, and they shall recover." (Mark 16:17-18)*

What an awesome privilege we have because of the blood of Jesus. (Hallelujah, praise the Lord!)

# CHAPTER TWENTY-TWO

# THE BLOOD OF JESUS WINS ARMAGEDDON

From the early nineties, I revisited the study of the power that's in the blood of Jesus. I found many more truths not yet explained that I decided to write a book hoping it would open the eyes of believers and unbelievers to the hidden powers in the blood of Jesus.

I believe it was the Holy Spirit that directed me to write this book. Since the unction for this book came, I have written and recorded many songs. The more I researched the blood of Jesus a greater desire came to write this book. Even now as I am writing the final chapter, I know that I have only tapped into a very small segment of the study of the blood of Jesus Christ.

However, of all the things that I have seen and researched there is nothing with the exception of our salvation, that is more powerful than what I am about to share with you.

From the sacrifice of Abel and all the slain animals by the priest to the cross of Jesus Christ where He became both priest and lamb, the blood of Jesus speaks. The cleansing of the lepers, the seven times Jesus shed his blood: from the garden of Gethsemane to the piercing of His side on Calvary; speak volumes of the power that is in the blood of Jesus.

From the sacrifices of animals each day by Job as a blood covering for his family, to the sacrificing of each animal by the children of Israel before they entered battles as a means of guaranteed victory, the blood of Jesus Christ stands victorious.

The celebration of all the feast of Israel, especially the Day of Atonement, to the slaughter of thousands of animals by King Solomon at the dedication of the temple continues to tell us that there is no redemption without the blood of Jesus.

I have examined quite a number of areas of the blood of Jesus, many of them you may have heard before. However, I want to conclude by drawing attention to one of the most powerful revelation I have ever received concerning the blood of Jesus.

I believe that the church of the Lord Jesus Christ will be raptured and then the world will experience the worst seven years that it has ever seen. This period is called the tribulation. Daniel called it Israel's seventieth week.

*"Seventy weeks are determined upon thy people and upon thy holy city, to finish the transgression, and to make an end of sins, and to make reconciliation for iniquity, and to bring in everlasting righteousness, and to seal up the vision and prophecy, and to anoint the most Holy." (Daniel 9:24)*

At the conclusion of the seventy weeks, the battle of Armageddon will be fought.

My purpose here is not to go into details concerning the seven years tribulation or the battle of Armageddon, but to show you how this battle is fought and won by Jesus' blood.

*"And I saw heaven opened, and behold a white horse; and He that sat upon him was called Faithful and True, and in righteousness He doth judge and make war. His eyes were as a flame of fire, and on His head were many crowns; and He had a name written, that no man knew, but He Himself. And He was clothed with a vesture dipped in blood: and His name is called The Word of God. And the armies which were in heaven followed Him upon white horses, clothed in fine linen, white and clean." (Revelation 19:11-14)*

This portion describes Jesus leaving heaven with all the resurrected saints following Him back to earth to fight the battle of Armageddon. Jesus again sends one of the most powerful messages concerning the power that is in His blood. Jesus is the Word and comes with a sharp sword (word) in His mouth. To see Him dip His garment in His own blood before coming back to fight tells me that there is absolutely no victory without the blood of Jesus.

If Jesus is using His own blood to cover Himself to go into battle, why would we fight the battles we are in today without the blood of Jesus Christ?

I believe that the blood of Jesus has lost its importance to many believers. It has become too old-fashioned for today's modern Christians.

In **Hebrew 13:8,** Jesus Christ is the same yesterday, today, and forever. I believe that this is the reason why we lack victory in many areas of our lives, especially where there are battles. No battle can be won without the blood of Jesus Christ.

There are people who would argue that the blood of Jesus was only applicable in the Old Testament. My answer to their arguments is in a form of a question. Why then did Jesus use it in the New Testament? He has left us to fight every battle He has already won; and we will win providing we use His blood.

The winning of the battle of Armageddon is His responsibility, and He comes back winning with His blood. Have you not wondered where the blood came from that He dipped His garment in?

**Hebrews 9:11-12** clearly shows that Jesus took His own blood into heaven and sprinkled the furniture in the Tabernacle there. This blood which has been in Heaven for over two thousand years is the same blood Jesus will dip His garment in before He returns to fight the battle of Armageddon.

Let us return to applying the blood every day over our own lives, the lives of our families, our possessions, churches, cities, countries, and the world. *He is still the Lamb of God that taketh away the sin of the world!*

**For additional information contact Rev. Rudolph K. Roberts**

**Mail Address:**     **P.O. Box F – 43699**
                         **Freeport, Grand Bahama**
                         **Bahamas**

**Office:**    **242-352-5420**
              **1-954-636-6309**

**Fax:**     **242-351-6034**

**Media Center:**    **242-352-5450**

**Home:**    **242-373-7516**
              **1-305-394-6177**

**Email:**    **revrudykrwmcc@hotmail.com**
              revrudykr@hotmail.com

LaVergne, TN USA
09 November 2009
163453LV00004B/2/P